Tassels & Trims

Exquisite Machine
Embroidery Projects

Quilters' Resource *publications*

Tassels & Trims

Editor: Susan Beck
Assistant Editor: Jo Leichte
Illustrations: Marthe Young
Photography: Jim Altobell, Altobell Imagery

First published in 2004 by Quilters' Resource, Inc.
P.O. Box 148850 · Chicago, IL 60614
(773) 278-5695

Text, machine embroidery designs, and project
designs ©2004 BERNINA® of America, Inc.

National Library of Congress
Meyer, Louisa   *Tassels & Trims*

ISBN 1-889682-41-1

Tassels & Trims

Louisa Meyer

From Kempton Park, South Africa, Louisa Meyer was introduced to sewing at a very early age with her own little chain stitch sewing machine. She used it to create the daintiest wedding dresses for anyone who owned a Barbie doll!

After finishing high school, she completed a two-year Diploma course in dress designing and tailoring through City And Guilds of London at the Industrial College for the Clothing Industry in Johannesburg. After graduating she designed christening, wedding and prom dresses for 20 years.

Then she found her new passion—digitizing! Two Tassel Collections have since been created and she taught an advanced embroidery class at BERNINA® University in Monterey CA., 2003. This passion led her to write this book and digitize a special collection of Tassels & Trims designs.

Apart from digtizing she still finds time to indulge in her first love—free-hand embroidery. New creations however persistently intrude into these adored pastimes insisting on being given space and time to be manifested as projects and designs!

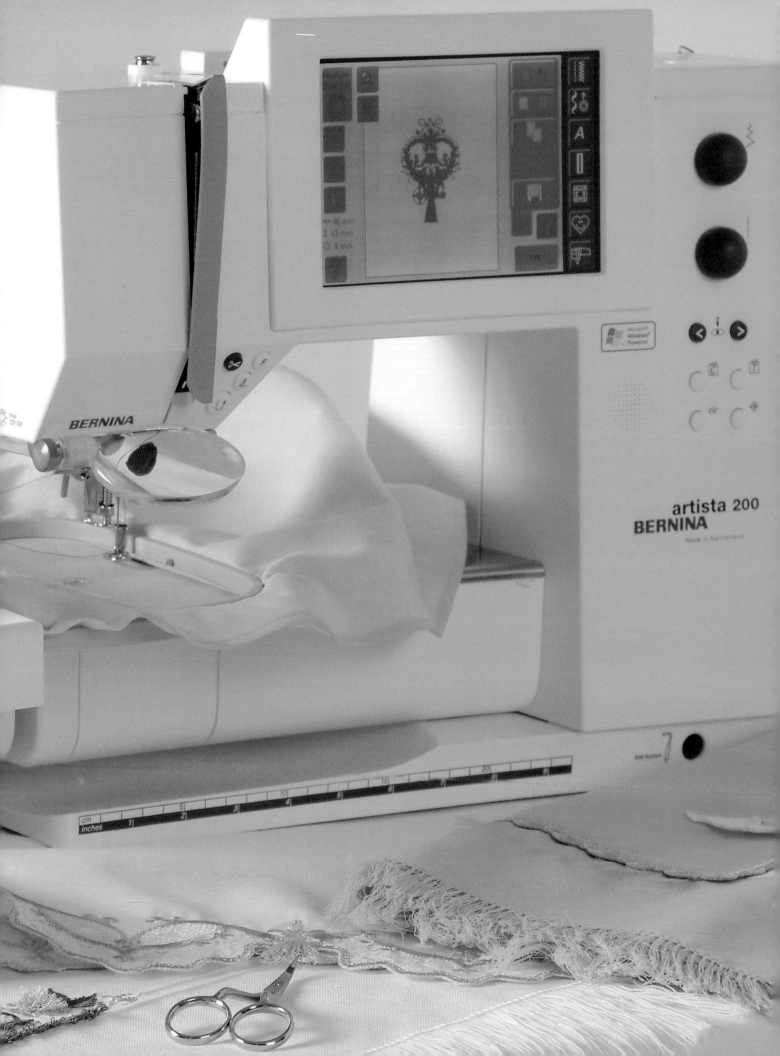

Producing *Tassels & Trims* with BERNINA® of America has been a once-in-a-lifetime experience. I'm so grateful to Dieter Bachor, Production Manager, BERNINA® Switzerland and Gayle Hillert, Vice President of Education, BERNINA® of America, for taking up the challenge with me. Since that first day of my visit to Steckborn, a picturesque little town next to Lake Constance (the new South African flag waving in front of the BERNINA® head office—especially for me!), it has been an incredible journey. I arrived with a few stitched tassel samples, a suitcase full of tassel projects, and a lot of hope.

The first tassels were created on the most basic of BERNINA® embroidery machines, the *Deco* 600, and digitized with the Wizard version 2 software. Not a lot of convincing was necessary once I had explained the tassel technique. I'm sure that it was the wonderful tassel projects that convinced them to give the final go-ahead for *Tassels & Trims*...and then it had to be a huge secret until the release of the first collection.

Acknowledgements

Before my trip to Switzerland, all my BERNINA® friends eagerly helped with stitching projects—cushions, a border on a curtain, and tray cloths. The boardroom table was covered with tassels! My sincere thanks to all these ladies; without whose first projects any of this would have been possible.

BERNINA® Dealers, Martie Muller, for stitching the border on the denim capri pants, Magaretha Engelbrecht, for all your support, and to Marissa Wulhuter for all your support.

Veronica Coetzee, the first friend with whom I shared my 3-dimensional tassel creation; she exclaimed, "Go for it!" Thanks for the silk tray cloth. Your effort ended as a preprogrammed motif on the *artista* 200E.

Martie Nieuwoudt for the beautiful pink cushion, Annetjie Norris for her place mat, Dalene Loretz's Christmas Candle, Mariette Potgieter for the curtain embroidery, and Esther Lukas for her table runner.

While the first collection—*Tassels & Trims I*—was created for the *Deco* embroidery, the second collection was created with the absolute top-of-the-range *artista* 200E and the BERNINA® Embroidery Software Version 4. Now, to top it all—*Tassels & Trims* "The BOOK"—plus a special collection of new designs with BERNINA® of America. In my wildest dreams I never thought it would be possible!

Once again, thank you Gayle, the "Tassels" were your "baby," and your staff so professional. Thanks to Susan Beck and Jo Leichte for the end result—all my creations in a book. After meeting you both I just knew this was going to be **BIG** with **The Best of the Best!**

And thanks to OESD and Tamara Fox for their hard work with the production of all the tassel collections—making the final product available in all embroidery formats.

And the people back home—
I needed a Dealer that could assist me with my new *artista* 200E. Leni Da Costa from BERNINA® East Rand Mall, and her staff, Amelia Bodenstein and Karen van Eden, assisted me through this book-writing experience with their sewing and embroidery expertise. They received me with open arms. When I needed a "pick-me-up", they were there.

More new BERNINA® friends stitched projects and edited instructions when I failed to express myself clearly. Lisa Brummer, a young embroidery and sewing enthusiast, and Johan Neehtling, both for all the testing and writing expertise. Suzette De Viliers tested patterns and stitched motifs.

Two very special ladies, Marilyn Hugelshofer from Switzerland for her workshops as far as Germany promoting the tassel collections, and Marlis Bennet, from BERNINA® of America, for all her wonderful tassel projects in *Designs in Machine Embroidery.*

BENARTEX for supplying me with all the wonderful floral fabrics for the Tasseled Quilt and coordinating pillow.

A special dedication to my husband Frikkie and my two sons Hannes and Jakkie for their incredible patience, support, and love. Thank you all!!

I am very fortunate in my career to be able to meet creative, talented people—but meeting Louisa Meyer was definitely a highlight in my life. When I first saw the tassels she had created in the software with her special technique, I was intrigued and impressed with the cleverness and beauty of the stitching. Then she showed me the creative application of her designs and I was excited at the possibilities.

Foreword

She created a tassel design that we could use as a preprogrammed design on the *artista* 200E so everyone who owned the machine could try a tassel. But then I thought, how many ways are there to sew a tassel? The answer is found in this beautiful book of inspiration. Louisa has taken her tassel technique to a new art form with projects and plans to fit every sewer's taste and lifestyle.

We like to talk about all the segments of sewing—garments, crafts, home dec, quilting and embroidery and Louisa's tassels fit nicely in all the segments. Most sewers don't confine themselves to one segment—we like to dally in all the areas of creating. This book will enable you to sew for yourself or your children, decorate your home with exquisite pillows, sew lovely gifts for your friends and family, use the technique with quilting and quilted clothing, and embroider to your heart's content.

Creating with sewing and embroidery systems provides a profound sense of satisfaction and enjoyment—the very act of embellishing beautiful fabrics with beautiful threads is a worthy pursuit. Louisa's designs make this pursuit even more inspirational because of the quality and artistry of her projects. Louisa's imagination seems to know no limits. I would pick up one of the projects she sent for inclusion in the book, shake my head in wonderment, think to myself, "There can be nothing to exceed this," then discover another project, shake my head in wonderment—and go through the same routine again.

I am amazed and awed by Louisa's talent, her sense of style and form, her playfulness and craftsmanship. And I am truly respectful of her excellence in all she does. Yes, her projects and tassels inspire—her workmanship and artfulness are inspirational. But, in reality, because of this book, embroidered tassels and trims are attainable for each and every sewer. We can all transform our fabrics with charming tassels and exquisite trims—and make our existence a little more beautiful. Thank you, Louisa, for your wonderful imagination, your willingness to share, your boundless energy and your sense of style.

And thank you, the sewer, for plunging into this journey of aesthetic finesse. I am sure your sewing existence will be enhanced as you stitch a tassel or two to decorate your life. Once you begin, it is hard to stop—enjoy!

Gayle Hillert
VP of Education/Training
BERNINA® of America, Inc.

Table of Contents

After years of creating embroidery on my sewing machine I had the opportunity to buy my first embroidery machine. Before that it took hours to create just one flower, building a single petal and leaf at a time and combining them with all the other decorative stitches on the machine.

Introduction

Could I ever imagine that I would be so fortunate to be part of all the new BERNINA® technology? With the *artista* 200E and the incredible BERNINA® embroidery software there's no limit to creating all these wonderful trims. I find inspiration for the trims everywhere around me and ideas just "happen." By chance I developed a new type of stitchery for the household embroidery machine—"Tassels & Trims"— exclusively for BERNINA®.

With this book I want to share my new tassel ideas as well as guide you through previous *Tassels & Trims* design collections. Use this book as a guide for these collections but do not let it stop you from creating your own projects. In these chapters there will be something for the novice, complete with patterns and full instructions. The experts will only need a picture or a new trim to spark new ideas of their own. This is the opportunity to dust off your tassel design collections, combine them with the new Special Collection, and start sewing these great new projects that you have been asking and waiting for. If you do not have the time to sew a new project, take out all those linens that have never been used and add a tassel border. Liven up the pillowcases with a single motif and repeat it on the towels. Spoil yourself before your friends or family see it!

A new dimension is added by applying continuous trims or by just adding a single tassel as an embellishment of home furnishings or garments. Experiment with the trims by using different threads and fabrics. Stitch samples following the instructions and it won't be long before you understand the process and versatility of combining and linking trims and tassels. No tassel or trim will be left unstitched, and you'll be creating heirloom pieces that will be cherished for years to come.

Please note that the machines and supplies listed for each product are those of BERNINA® of America, Inc. and its sister companies: Oklahoma Embroidery Supply and Design, Quilter's Resource, Inc., and Benartex Fabrics. The designs can be stitched on other brands of embroidery machines using the appropriate format. For the best results, use a similar hoop size as listed in the supplies section of each project (refer to page 12 for these sizes). Whenever possible, the specific stabilizers, threads, and supplies should be used as listed; however, if they are not available, the type of product is listed as well as the brand name so you can substitute what is available in your area.

Add tactile interest and visual drama
to almost anything—furniture,
clothing, accessories, draperies—
by attaching rich tassels and trims.

A Rich Embellishment

In use for over 5,000 years, tassels have a long and varied history. They can be traced back to weavers of nomadic tribes who tied the threads of garments, rugs and blankets, controlling them to prevent fraying, thus resulting in a tassel. In ancient Egypt fringes and tassels have been found in the royal tombs and an early form of the tassel is referred to in the Bible. While tassels started as a practical answer to a weaving problem, they have few uses today other than embellishment and decoration.

More than one culture has used tassels to denote power, status, and wealth. The ancient Chinese wore tassels as a sign of nobility and during Renaissance times, the Catholic Church used tassels to define their hierarchy. During medieval times braid makers created intricate decorations for domestic use, furnishings, ceremonial and military wear.

The French perfected the art of tassel making, becoming masters of "passementerie"— a general term for tassels, fringe and trims of all sorts. In France, using tassels reached its height during the reign of Louis XIV. Tassels in all shapes and sizes, made of silk, cotton, and wool were used to adorn everything from clothing and homes to horses and carriages, signifying wealth, power, and style. Later, Napoleon's throne was decorated with gold tassels.

During the Victorian and Edwardian eras, interior décor items such as sofas, pillows, curtains and pictures were richly decorated in every possible way, and tassels once again moved to the forefront of embellishment.

As a design element, tassels move in and out of style, and reappearing as symbols of richness and luxuriance. They were popular in the Art Nouveau period of the early twentieth century when synthetics such as rayon in vibrant colors were introduced. During World War II elaborate decorating was scaled down, and by the 1960's only a few family-run businesses continued the art of tassel making.

And now in the 21st Century, combining traditional influences with state-of-the-art technology, BERNINA® of America, Inc. has given us the tools to create a new style of tassels using computer software and the household embroidery machine. Embroidery by machine has introduced an entirely new element to the home sewer and crafter. Not only can rich designs be stitched onto all types of projects, but, with digitizing software, original designs can be created and unusual techniques can be used. The tassel designs shown in this book start with a stitched design, but with some specific clipping and trimming techniques they become three dimensional, adding new levels of tactile and visual interest. The designs in the *Tassels and Trims* collections can be used as single designs or, with precise placement and hooping techniques, can also be used as trims, free hanging borders, and corner motifs. These unique designs are easy to stitch and give us the opportunity to create our own heirloom pieces—building history for the future.

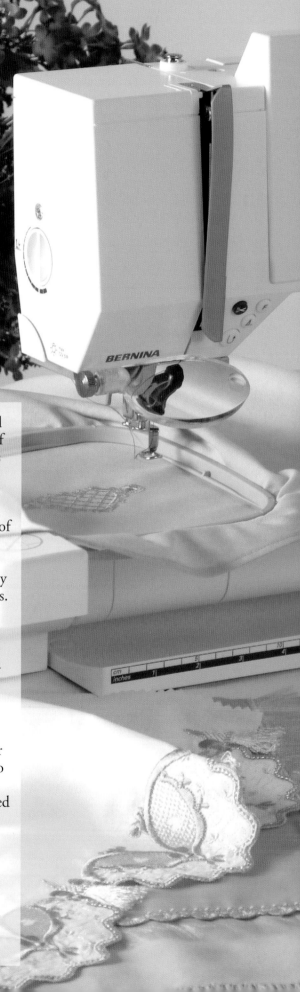

The following glossary defines vocabulary terms that are fundamental to embroidery by machine and to the Tassels & Trims designs found in Collection I, Collection II, and the Special Collection included with this book.

Terms & Techniques

Appliqué
A technique of "applying" cloth shapes to a background fabric, appliqué is a way of achieving a large area of color in an embroidery design without using a large number of stitches.

Backing
A fibrous or paper-like material used to stabilize fabric for embroidery. For best results, backings are temporarily bonded to and hooped with the fabric. Called "stabilizer" in home sewing and embroidery terms, this indispensable product comes in cut-away, tear-away, burn-away, and water-soluble forms. Available in a variety of weights, backings can be fusible, adhesive-backed, or plain. The most common color is white, with some types available in black and beige.

Bobbin Thread
Thread that comes off the bobbin and forms the back of an embroidery design. When stitching tassel designs, the bobbin thread behind each tassel is clipped to let the needle thread hang loose, forming the "skirt" of the tassel. A lightweight thread is often used on the bobbin to minimize the bulk of the stitching. Fine polyester bobbin thread is available in large cones of black and white. Other fine threads can also be used such as 60-weight cotton, which is readily available in a wide range of colors.

Border Trim
A continuous embroidery design typically used along the edge of a project, such as a tablecloth, curtain or valance, skirt hem, center placket, etc. Borders may be stitched directly on the fabric edge or embroidered on polyester organdy, trimmed, and applied to the edge in the same manner as purchased trim yardage. If stitched on the fabric, the edge below the stitched border can be finished with conventional hemming techniques such as a turned or rolled hem, or the fabric can be trimmed from around the lower edge of the design, leaving a shaped edge on the project.

chapter 2

Digitizing

The art of digitally converting artwork from paper or graphic form into a format that can be used to stitch embroidery. This is done via embroidery software using a mouse to manipulate graphic art on the computer screen. The digitizer creates a computer file that "tells" the embroidery machine when and where to stitch, as well as what kind of stitch to use and the specifics of the stitch attributes (such as density and length). Just as files on the computer consist of pixels (dots per inch), digitized embroidery files consist of a series of stitch points that direct the sewing computer to move the embroidery hoop back and forth and side to side, forming the design as the needle stitches.

Embroidery Thread

Available in a variety of weights and fibers, each type of machine embroidery thread has its advantages and disadvantages. Most home embroiderers use a variety of types, tailoring thread selection to the particular fabric or project at hand. The most common types are polyester, rayon, cotton, and metallic, but are also available in acrylic, wool, silk and other fibers. They come in a wide range of colors including variegated and twisted colors, and in weights from very fine to heavy. For more information on thread, consult the chart on page 22.

Embroidery Wand

Small tool used to "lift" embroidery stitches for trimming. Also used to pull thread tails to the back side of a project/fabric.

Fill Stitch
A fill stitch covers large areas of an embroidery design, and might be described as "coloring inside the lines". The simplest fill stitch is a satin stitch, but computerized machines can fill areas with "step" stitches that can be programmed as designs or patterns. Dozens of automatic fill stitches are available in embroidery software programs and new ones can be created using digitizing software.

Freestanding Appliqué
An embroidery design stitched on water-soluble stabilizer (Aqua Film, Badgemaster), organza, netting, or other material that will be removed, trimmed, or burned from the outside edges of the design, leaving a "freestanding" motif that can be appliquéd to a project. *Note: Not all embroidery designs are suitable for stitching on water-soluble stabilizers; they must be specially digitized so that the stitches interlock and do not separate when the stabilizer is rinsed away.*

Hooping
One of the most important aspects of machine embroidery, hooping holds the fabric and stabilizer taut so the design can stitch evenly and perfectly. Home embroidery machines come with hoops of different sizes that are made to fit particular machines. For best results, always use the smallest hoop that will accommodate the selected embroidery motif. This provides the most support for the fabric and helps prevent flagging (fabric moving up and down the needle).

Jump Stitches
Stitches that are formed when the needle travels from the last stitch of one section to the first stitch of the next section. Jump stitches should be clipped after each color is embroidered to keep them from being trapped under successive stitching and embedded in the design.

Medallion Design
A single design, or group of designs combined to form one visual unit. Typically used at the center of a cushion, tablecloth, etc. May be as simple as a floral wreath of blossoms arranged in a circle, or as complex as an arrangement of intertwining designs.

Mega Hoop
Extra large hoop for the BERNINA® *artista* 200E that allows a very large design to be stitched without rehooping. Many home embroidery machines have some type of large hoop. Others are multi-positional and require the hoop to be moved from position to position to stitch all the parts of the design. The *artista* 200E automatically splits large designs for the multiple positions of the Mega Hoop; other multi-position hoops may require the user to manually split the design for the different positions.

Outline Stitch
Outline stitches may be used to define individual portions of a design or sewn around the entire design to sharpen and define the edges. Typically formed using straight or satin stitches, decorative stitches such as feather or blanket stitches may also be used to create outlines.

Pattern Stitch
Stitches that imitate the decorative stitches of the sewing machine; they can be used as outlines, appliqué edges and openwork fills.

Satin Stitch
Zigzag stitches placed close together, side by side, to create outlines or to fill large areas of embroidery designs. Satin stitches create a smooth surface with subtle shine, resembling the reflective woven surface of satin fabric.

Stabilizer
Also known as backing, this product is used to stabilize fabric before stitching designs on it. The type of stabilizer used on a particular project is dependent on several factors such as type of fabric, thread, intended use, and stitch density. Dense designs need an adequate base to support the stitches through use, washing, etc. and require the use of a permanent stabilizer such as cut-away. Openwork and other less dense designs require only temporary support during the stitching process as provided by tear-away or water-soluble types of backings. For more information on stabilizers, consult the chart on page 23.

Template
  Paper Templates - Drawings or photos (actual size) of embroidery designs that are included with the collections. These are used to determine and mark the placement of designs on fabric. They can also be printed for designs created using BERNINA® embroidery software.

  Plastic Hoop Templates - Clear, gridded plastic sheets that fit inside the inner embroidery hoops and are used for positioning embroidery designs before stitching. Always remove the plastic hoop template before beginning to stitch!

Using the correct tools and supplies ensures that the stitching process is smooth and the results beautiful. The following pages detail the items that have been used to stitch the Tassels and Trims designs and projects featured in this book.

Materials & Supplies

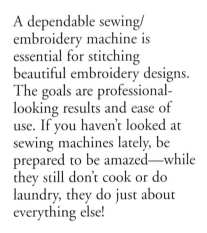

A dependable sewing/ embroidery machine is essential for stitching beautiful embroidery designs. The goals are professional-looking results and ease of use. If you haven't looked at sewing machines lately, be prepared to be amazed—while they still don't cook or do laundry, they do just about everything else!

Today's embroidery machines have lots of great features—on-screen editing, resizing and rescaling, mirror image, and rotating—that make placing and positioning the designs exactly as you want simple to accomplish. Completely computerized, these amazing machines are not only easy to use but result in highly professional stitched designs. One of the most important "features" you should look for is a dealer who offers information and inspiration so you can get the most from your machine.

Embroidery machines for home use have been on the market since the late 1980s and have evolved into two types: stand-alone embroidery machines that simply stitch digitized embroidery designs but do not have sewing capabilities and combination machines that stitch designs and offer sewing machine functions as well.

Having separate embroidery and sewing machines can be convenient, as both can be used simultaneously. If you are a frequent sewer or sew on multiple projects at the same time, you may want two separate machines. One consideration is the space you have available for machines. Obviously you will need room for both, and ideally they should be in fairly close proximity (in the same room) to each other for convenience in moving back and forth between the two. Usually, a stand-alone embroidery machine is less expensive than a complete sewing/embroidery system. An example of a quality stand-alone embroidery machine is the Bernette® for BERNINA® *Deco* machine. This workhorse of an embroidery machine offers quality stitching and simple operation.

On the other hand, a complete sewing and embroidery system may offer you the best scenario for your particular sewing situation. If you don't have room for two machines, a combination unit takes up less space and offers the features and functions of both types of machines. Most sewing machine manufacturers offer embroidery as an add-on option to their top-of-the-line sewing machines, with fully loaded feature packages on both parts of the system. The BERNINA® *artista*, available in three models—the 200E, 185QEE, and the 165E Heritage Edition—is an example of a complete sewing/embroidery system and offers every feature available to the home embroiderer.

BERNINA® Embroidery Software, version 4

Use the software to combine images and to print paper templates indicating placement of embroidery motifs in a medallion or border. There are three software packages from which to choose:

Editor–Powerful but easy to use software for making changes to existing designs.

Auto-Designer–An easy way to create professional looking embroidery designs from artwork in seconds. The program includes BERNINA® Quilter, Cross Stitch and PhotoSnap.

Designer Plus–Explore the complete world of embroidery software including BERNINA® Quilter, hand look craft stitches, Cross Stitch, PhotoSnap, auto appliqué, auto digitizing and manual digitizing tools.

Customized Pattern Selection Software (optional)

Available for BERNINA® *virtuosa* and *artista* sewing and embroidery systems, the CPS software allows the user to change the decorative stitches and embroidery designs programmed into the sewing machine or embroidery module.

OESD Explorations Software (optional)

A wonderful tool for planning and viewing embroidery designs on clothing, home dec, crafts, and other projects. Use this software for creating your own tassels and trims projects.

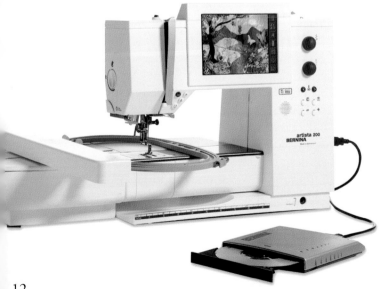

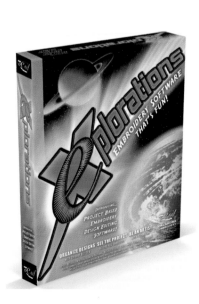

Studio BERNINA® Tassels & Trims embroidery collections

Collection I–The original Tassels & Trims collection by Louisa Meyer, this collection of over 100 designs is available at your local BERNINA® dealer or at www.embroideryonline.com.

Collection II–Also designed by Louisa, this design collection has over 100 designs and is available at your local BERNINA® dealer or at www.embroideryonline.com.

Special Collection CD–A special mini collection of 57 designs, these designs by Louisa are only available on the CD included with this book; all designs are provided in the most popular home embroidery formats.

Magic Box & Magic Card (optional)

The Magic Box allows designs to be downloaded from the BERNINA® embroidery software to almost any brand embroidery machine, including Bernette® *Deco*/BabyLock/Brother, Elna/Janome/New Home/Kenmore, Pfaff, Simplicity, Singer, and Viking. In addition, it also reads non-*artista* embroidery cards and allows them to be used with the *artista* and/or *Deco* embroidery systems.

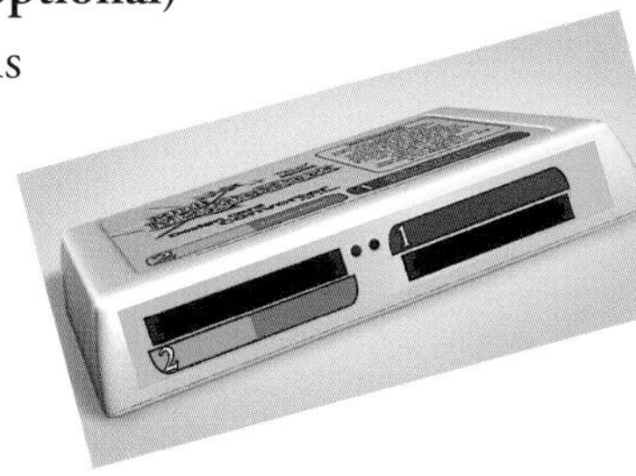

Reader/Writer and Personal Design Card (optional)

Use the *artista* Card Reader/Writer and an *artista* Personal Design Card to copy designs to and from your *artista* and PC.

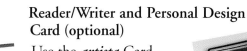

Embroidery Hoops
artista Embroidery Hoops

Note: Always use a hoop size that closely matches your design size to provide better fabric control, and better finished results.

Small/Free Arm (optional accessory for 165E)–Use this hoop for small designs. Perfect for miniatures and for detail work on cuffs and collars. This hoop is recommended for use with the BERNINA® Exclusive Free Arm Embroidery Spacer.

Free Arm Embroidery Spacer (optional for artista 165E)–Use this device with the Small *artista* embroidery hoop to embroider hard-to-reach areas such as sleeve cuffs, pant legs, etc.

Medium–Use this hoop for mid-size designs, measuring 50–110mm wide and 50–130mm tall.

Large (165E/170E/180E)–Use this hoop for large designs and design combinations. Ideal for combining mid-sized to large designs with lettering.

Large Oval (185E/200E only)–The oval shape of this hoop eliminates corner areas, offering more usable space within the hoop.

Hoop Size	Stitching Field	Hoop Size	Stitching Field
***artista* Hoops**		***Deco* 650 Hoops**	
Small/Free Arm	72mm x 50mm = 2" x 1⅞"	Extra Small	30mm x 50mm = 1⅛" x 2"
Medium	110mm x 130mm = 4¼" x 1⅛"	Small	70mm x 70mm = 2¾" x 2¾"
Large	155mm x 200mm = 6⅛" x 7⅞"	Medium (Regular)	110mm x 110mm = 4¼" x 4¼"
Large Oval	145mm x 255mm = 5¾" x 10"	Large (3-Position)	100mm x 172mm = 3⅞" x 6¾"
Mega	150mm x 400mm = 5⅞" x 15¾"	***Deco* 330 Hoops**	
		Small	50mm x 50mm = 1⅞" x 1⅞"
		Medium	110mm x 126mm = 4¼" x 5"
		Large	140mm x 200mm = 5½" x 7⅞"

Mega (artista 200E only)–This three-position embroidery hoop is designed to stitch extra large designs up to 150mm x 400mm. Designs created using *artista* software can be sent to the *artista* where the Art Engine of the machine will automatically split the design into the appropriate sections for stitching.

Deco Embroidery Hoops

Extra Small/Cuffs & Collars–This extra small hoop is designed to fit in areas where a conventional hoop won't, such as collars, cuffs and pockets. Use when stitching very small designs such as small monograms.

Small–Use this small hoop for better fabric control when stitching smaller designs.

Medium–This medium size hoop will accommodate a wide variety of designs for your *Deco*. The positioning template allows you to hoop the fabric for exact stitch placement.

Large–Create large-sized combinations on your *Deco* embroidery machine. Up to three designs can be combined. The hoop is easily repositioned thanks to a simple 3-position clip.

Accessories

Multi-spool Thread Stand–(*Deco & artista*) Save time when embroidering! Organize and arrange thread colors in the order they are needed and they'll be ready and waiting as you stitch through your design. This convenient spool holder will accommodate conventional spools as well as cones. Also available: Add-on extensions with extra spool holders.

Magnifier Set–Get a close up look of your work with these magnifying glasses. This set of three lenses offers varying degrees of magnification to suit your needs. Use these magnifiers to facilitate needle threading, for precision work, etc. Also included is a handle for converting to a hand-held magnifier.

Plexiglas™ Tables–Need extra support for large embroidery projects? This extended sewing surface is 24" x 24", features heavy Plexiglas™ construction, and fits around the embroidery module of your BERNINA® embroidery machine. Five legs provide sturdy support and are easily removed for storage. The slick surface allows uninhibited movement of fabric, necessary for successful embroidery. A static-cling ruler, with both metric and inch markings, can be positioned anywhere on the surface of the table.

Straight Stitch Plate–This stitch plate promotes perfect stitch quality when embroidering, as the small needle hole provides fabric support all around the needle as each stitch is formed.

Thread Nets–Useful for preventing slippery threads from unwinding too quickly and/or tangling.

Spool Caps–Used to keep thread spools in place on spool pins, and also to prevent threads from catching at ends of spools. Use the correct size for the thread spool.

Presser Foot–Using the correct presser foot for each sewing task not only makes the job easier to accomplish but also gives more professional-looking results. The feet listed here are ones used to make the projects detailed in Chapters 7–10 of this book.

Embroidery Foot #15–for embroidery with the *artista* embroidery module

Edgestitch Foot #10/10C–for edgestitching, understitching, hems

Open Embroidery Foot #20/20C–for satin stitch embroidery

Clear Appliqué Foot #23–for making and inserting mini-piping; for satin stitch appliqué

Pintuck Foot #31–for double needle raised tucks

Clear Foot #34/34C–for seaming and decorative stitching

Scissors–The importance of trimming and clipping in relation to embroidery is often overlooked but can make the difference between a beautiful finished design and a "so-so" stitchout. Good scissors are especially important for the techniques in this book as clipping the bobbin threads and trimming the tassels are what give life to the designs. There are several types from which to choose and specific situations in which to use each one.

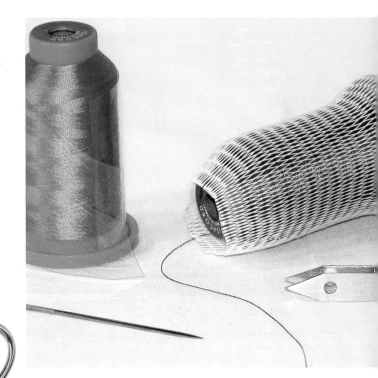

Appliqué–Angled handle makes trimming more comfortable; "duck bill" design lifts the fabric being trimmed while keeping fabric underneath from accidentally being snipped. Perfect for appliqué, heirloom sewing, trimming seam allowances.

Blunt Point Embroidery Scissors–Sharp blades cut fabric easily, while blunt point prevents accidentally snipping through fabric.

Curved Blade Embroidery Scissors–Curved blades and/or handles improves ability to cut in awkward places, such as trimming threads from fabric mounted in embroidery hoop.

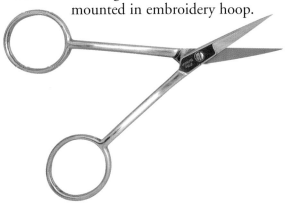

Snips–3¹/₂" "Easy Cut", spring-loaded ("squeeze" type) scissor reduces hand fatigue while snipping threads smoothly; ergonomic, ambidextrous design, constructed of lightweight stainless steel.

Notions–Small items and gadgets can make sewing and embroidering easier by helping with specific tasks that may be tedious or time consuming. The notions listed here are ones used in making the projects detailed in Chapters 7–10 of this book.

Embroidery Wand–Useful for pulling thread to the back (or front) of the work; especially nice for working with tassels and fringe. Bonus: Also great for pulling snagged sweater stitches to the wrong side.

Thread Nets–Useful for preventing slippery threads from unwinding too quickly and/or tangling.

Amazing Tape–Wrap a length of this "self-stick" plastic around spools to keep threads from unwinding when stored.

Bobbinsaver–Just the thing for keeping bobbins corralled and ready to use. *TIP: Wind several bobbins at the start of a project, then store them in the Bobbinsaver; they'll be ready when needed, without becoming a mass of tangled threads.*

Uncle Bill's Tweezers–Precision points and spring-tempered stainless steel make these the best tweezers for gripping wayward threads. Bonus: Also great for removing slivers.

Even the most exquisite embroidery can lose appeal when stitched improperly. That's why it's important to develop good hooping techniques and to use appropriate stabilizers in proper ways.

Perfect Projects

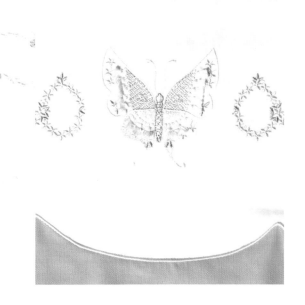

Beautiful embroidery designs are the result of creative ideas that develop into imaginative artwork ready to be digitized. The skill of the digitizer is one of the most important elements necessary for creating stunning embroidery. It not only takes knowledge of digitizing techniques but also an artistic eye to produce appealing stitched motifs. From planning the path of the needle and minimizing the number of jump threads to selecting the fill patterns and outline stitches, the skill of the digitizer has a great impact on whether a design is successful or not. Because of this, it is important to look for designs from reputable design houses that stand behind their work. Oklahoma Embroidery Supply and Design (OESD) has thousands of designs available at www.embroideryonline.com that are professionally digitized and ready to stitch for beautiful results.

Designs can be stitched with quality results only if the proper steps are taken to prepare the fabric and set up the machine. The elements that need the most critical attention are stabilizers or backing, needles, and threads. The right combination of these, plus correct hooping techniques, will help ensure beautiful embroidery results. The beginner or novice embroiderer who has not learned the importance of developing proper embroidery techniques will find problems such as designs with parts that do not align properly, outlines that are mismatched, and/or fabric that puckers around the stitched design after it is released from thc hoop. A common mistake that inexperienced stitchers often make is to blame the quality of the design for these failures, but once the relationship of the preparation steps to the finished design is understood it is easy to stitch beautiful designs every time. To eliminate or avoid these and other problems, familiarize yourself with the information on the following pages; it will soon be "second nature" and your stitched designs will always be perfect.

No matter which designs you select, a "practice run" is recommended to check your combination of fabric, thread, needle, and stabilizer. Spending a few extra minutes on this step will save you a great deal of time and supplies during the stitching and construction of your project. For best results, the test should be stitched on the same materials you have selected for your project. Paper or plastic templates can be used to ensure proper positioning and placement of designs, but only stitching a test swatch will help avoid possible problems with your choice of materials.

Basic Hooping Directions

Mark the center of the selected design on the fabric or garment. Draw horizontal and vertical lines through the center marking; keep these lines parallel and perpendicular to the lines of the plastic hoop template to prevent rotation of the fabric and skewed embroidery.

Place the appropriate stabilizer behind the fabric; bond layers using temporary spray adhesive, if needed.

Place the outer hoop on a hard, flat surface. Loosen the screw on the edge of the hoop.

Lay the stabilized fabric over the *outer* hoop, aligning the guidelines with the center markings on the edges of the hoops (•). Press the inner hoop into position over the fabric and check to see that the vertical and horizontal guidelines are parallel.
Note: Most hoops have center markings along the inner and outer edges. If not, create your own with a permanent ink marker.

Gently smooth the fabric, tightening the screw to hold it in place. Keep the marked guidelines straight to avoid distorting the grain of the fabric. The template provided with the hoop can be used to check the alignment. *Note: The fabric should be smooth and taut in the hoop but should not be stretched or distorted as this will cause puckers around the stitched design once it is released from the hoop.*

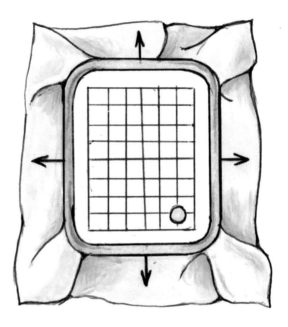

Many of the designs used for the projects in Chapters 7–10 have layers of embroidery stitched on top of each other, with 3-D tassels, tufts or fringed flowers providing extra texture and dimension. Final touches include heavy raised satin stitches, triple straight stitching and/or the daintiest French knots. Some motifs start as single designs, then were linked to form continuous borders or combined to make larger designs; after being embroidered they all come to life when the tassels are trimmed! To make sure your tassels and trims are perfect, observe the guidelines on the following pages.

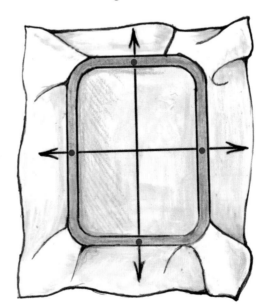

At the Beginning

Before starting any of the projects in this book, please read and look through all of the instructions, patterns and templates provided. This will enable you to plan ahead and anticipate the steps you need to follow for a satisfying sewing experience.

Start with a fresh piece of fabric:

- Always preshrink and press the fabric before starting a project.
- Steam the fabric to remove any folds or creases.
- Some fabrics can be spray starched, which will help stabilize them. This is especially useful for sheer fabrics such as organza and voile.

Select fabrics carefully. Correct choices of fabrics play an important role when making selections for a tassel project.

Stitch a sample of the trim or tassel first! This is very important so you can become familiar with the technique. An expensive project can be ruined when easily avoidable problems occur during the embroidering and construction phases. Fabrics, trims, needles and colors can easily be changed at the "sample stage" to ensure that your precious keepsake or heirloom piece is successfully completed.

When changing the embroidery thread colors of a motif to suit your personal taste, select them during daytime in natural light for the truest choices. Even the slightest change in color combination can affect the end result.

Positioning and Placement

Always baste or mark a guideline on the project before beginning embroidery. This will ensure the correct placement of the motifs, especially when linking them to create a continuous border. When re-hooping for a border, use the guideline on the project to re-center the hoop with the template to accurately link and continue the embroidery.

Use the motif templates supplied with each collection and check transferred positions during re-hoopings. Fabric can stretch after several hoopings so check the position each time and re-center if necessary. *Note: The templates for the Special Collection provided with this book can be printed from the enclosed CD.*

The Right Size

The tassels in both the first and second *Tassels & Trims* collections, as well as the Special Collection included

with this book, are digitized to stitch at the optimum size. For best results, BERNINA® of America, Inc., does not recommend resizing these designs. If you do change the size of these designs, always sew a test sample before embroidering on your garment or project. *Note: If changing the size of designs with long tassels on the Special Collection CD, artista 200E users must use the RESIZE option, as the RESCALE function cannot properly recalculate the stitches in the long tassels.*

Special Effects

Tips for Stitching Trims with Metallic Thread

- Always change to a larger needle—Embroidery needle #90/14 usually does the trick.
- Use a slower machine speed or embroider manually using the foot control.
- Stitch only the detail, or one layer, instead of the complete tassel using metallic thread. This will be easier on the machine and the fabric. This technique is explained in the instructions for sewing the valance in Chapter 9.

Tips for Stitching Heavy or Multiple Layer Tassels

- A slower machine speed works best when using wool and/or acrylic threads.
- Add an extra layer of stabilizer underneath the hoop before stitching the stage when the long satin stitches are formed. This extra stabilizer helps support the heavier stitching, prevents tunneling, and aids in cutting multi-layer tassels.

Problem Solving

If the fabric starts to pull underneath tassels:

- Add more stabilizer; sometimes multiple layers of a lightweight stabilizer work better than one layer of a heavyweight stabilizer and can be easier to remove.
- Make sure the hooped fabric is smooth and taut, but not stretched or distorted.
- If this occurs when using the Mega Hoop, add more clips to the sides of the hoop, especially the center sections. Medium size clipboard or binder clips can be used to supplement the clips packed with the Mega Hoop. Take care that they don't get in the way of the needle when the embroidery is stitching close to the sides.

If the fabric shows needle marks:

- Remove any penetration marks left on the fabric after the threads have been loosened on the front; lightly scratch the fabric threads with your fingernail or use the Embroidery Wand to restore the threads to their proper alignment. Steam press.

After the Stitching

- Take your time when cutting or removing the bobbin threads on the back of the tassel embroidery. This is a crucial stage, as the embroidery underneath can be damaged if threads are incorrectly clipped. See Chapter 5 for specific clipping and trimming techniques.

- Remove all of the unneeded stabilizer from the back after stitching is complete. Take care when removing it around the stitches as the reinforcing stitches can be damaged and cause the tassels to fall apart. Fabric can be easily damaged as well.

Needles

Type	Brand	Sizes—Uses—Comments
Universal Used for most fabrics including wovens and some knits; slightly rounded point (compromise between Sharp and Ballpoint) to stitch between fibers rather than through them.	• BERNINA/Baumann • Schmetz	• #60/8—fine wovens (batiste) • #70/10—medium to fine wovens (broadcloth) • #80/12—medium to heavy wovens (trigger, gabardine) • #90/14—heavy wovens (canvas, twill, upholstery) • #100/16, #110/18, #120/20—very heavy canvas, twill
Ball Point (H-SUK & H-SES) Rounded point penetrates between—rather than through—fabric yarns, preventing damage to knit fabrics.	• BERNINA/Baumann • Schmetz • Organ Embroidery *Organ eyes are a size larger than typical Embroidery needles, allowing threads to pass through the needle without fraying or snapping.*	• #70/10—fine knits (jersey) • #75/11—medium to fine knits (pique, jersey) • #80/12—medium to heavy knits (interlock, fleece) • #90/14—heavyweight knits (velour, heavy fleece) *Option: Titanium—5 times longer life than chromium plated needles.*
Microtex/Sharp (H-M) Sharp point penetrates fabric yarns, producing extremely accurate stitch placement; for silk and microfibers; also excellent for heirloom sewing and other techniques requiring a perfect straight stitch.	• BERNINA/Baumann • Schmetz Microtex Sharp • Organ Embroidery *Organ eyes are a size larger than typical Embroidery needles, allowing threads to pass through the needle without fraying or snapping.*	• #60/8—very fine wovens (silk, linen, batitse, microfiber) • #70/10—fine wovens (satin, silk, linen, batiste) • #75/11—medium to fine wovens (cotton, cotton/poly) • #80/12—medium to heavy wovens (chambray, trigger) • #90/14—heavy wovens (canvas, denim) *Option: Titanium—5 times longer life than chromium plated needles.*
Jeans/Denim (H-J) Sharp point for penetrating denim, plus stiff shaft to prevent bending and breaking. Large eye for accommodating topstitching thread.	• BERNINA/Baumann • Schmetz	• #70/10—lightweight denim, corduroy • #80/12—medium to heavy denim, artificial leather • #90/14—canvas, sailcloth, denim, artificial leather • #100/16—heavy canvas, sailcloth, denim, faux leather • #110/18—heavy canvas, sailcloth, denim, faux leather Also available: 4.0/100, 6.0/100 & 8.0/100 Twin Jeans
Metallic (H-MET & H-Metafil) Designed to prevent abrasion of delicate metallic threads.	• BERNINA/Baumann • Schmetz (Metallica) • Lammertz (Metafil)	• #70/10—fine knits (jersey) • #80/12—metallic threads • #90/14—heavyweight knits (velour, heavy fleece) Also available: 2.0/80 & 3.0/80 Twin Metallic
Embroidery (H-E) Sharp, with a large eye and groove, plus special coating and large scarf; prevents abrasion and shredding of delicate threads, especially metallics and rayons.	• BERNINA/Baumann • Schmetz Embroidery • Organ Embroidery *Organ eyes are a size larger than typical Embroidery needles, allowing threads to pass through the needle without fraying or snapping.*	• #70/10—lightweight threads & fabrics • #75/11—light to medium weight threads & fabrics • #80/12—medium weight threads & fabrics • #90/14—medium to heavyweight threads & fabrics *Option: Titanium—5 times longer life than chromium plated needles.* Also available: 2.0/75 & 3.0/75 Double Embroidery
Topstitching (H-N) Designed for use with heavy threads; very stiff to prevent excessive flexing when penetrating dense fabrics.	• BERNINA/Baumann • Schmetz	• #80/12—medium weight threads • #90/14—heavyweight threads • #110/16—very heavyweight threads
Double/Twin (ZWI) **& Triple/Drilling (DRI)** Two or three needles attached to one shank; includes Universal Double, Universal Triple/Drilling, Jeans Double, Twin Embroidery, Metallic Double	• BERNINA/Baumann • Schmetz	*Note: 1st number refers to distance (millimeters) between needles* • 1.6/70 • 3.0/75 • 6.0/100 • 1.6/80 • 3.0/80 • 8.0/100 • 2.0/75 • 3.0/90 • 2.0/80 • 4.0/80 • Triple 2.5/80 • 2.5/80 • 4.0/100 • Triple 3.0/80
Wing (H-Wing) Sharp point with a non-cutting wedge (wing) on each side; each stitch creates a small hole in the fabric without cutting; for hemstitching.	• BERNINA/Baumann • Schmetz	• #100/16—(linen, linen blends, heirloom stitching) • #120/18—(linen, linen blends, heirloom stitching)
Quilting (H-Q) Thin, tapered point for stitching through multiple layers of quilt fabrics	• BERNINA/Baumann • Schmetz	• #75/11—medium weight cottons; piecing, quilting • #90/14—heavyweight cottons; piecing, quilting
Stretch (H-S) Rounded point similar to ball point; designed for stitching elastic fabrics.	• BERNINA/Baumann • Schmetz	• #75/11—lightweight elastic knits (jersey, swimwear) • #90/14—heavyweight elastic knits (jersey, swimwear)

Thread

Type	Name/Brand	Uses—Comments
Polyester	• Isacord (OESD) • Metrosheen (Mettler) • Highlights (Superior Threads) • Rainbow Variegated (Superior Threads) • Highlights (Superior Threads)	• shiny finish • very strong, resists breaking • long-wearing; resists abrasion • doesn't bleed or fade • solid & variegated colors available
Cotton	• 60 wt cotton embroidery thread (Mettler) • 30 wt cotton embroidery thread (Mettler) • 50 wt cotton quilting thread (Mettler) • Colours 30 wt cotton quilting thread (YLI) • Select 50 wt cotton quilting thread (YLI) • Variegated cotton quilting thread (YLI) • King Tut 40 wt quilting (Superior Threads) • Perfect Quilting 30 wt (Superior Threads) • 30 wt cotton embroidery thread (Sulky) • 50 wt cotton Mako (Aurifil) • Cotona 80 (Madeira)	• matte finish • soft, lightweight • available in a variety of weights • 60 & 80 weights especially nice for heirloom projects • solid & variegated colors available
Metallic	• Yenmet (OESD) • Fine Metallic (YLI) • Reflections (YLI) • Metallic (Mettler) • Superior Metallic (Superior Threads) • Metallic 40 (Madeira)	• metallic shine • solid & variegated colors available • always use a special needle for metallic threads
Rayon	• 30 wt rayon embroidery thread (Sulky) • 40 wt rayon embroidery thread (Sulky) • Ultra Twist (Sulky) • Rayon 40 (Madeira)	• shiny finish • soft, lightweight, delicate • available in a variety of weights • especially nice for heirloom projects • solid, variegated, and twisted colors available
Acrylic	• Ultrasheen (YLI)	• shiny finish • very strong, resists breaking • long-wearing; resists abrasion • doesn't bleed or fade
Wool/Acrylic	• Monet (YLI)	• fuzzy, matte finish
Silk	• YLI Silk Thread	• shiny finish
Bobbin Thread	• Bobbin Thread (OESD) • 60 wt cotton embroidery thread (Mettler) • Lingerie & Bobbin (YLI) • The Bottom Line (Superior Threads)	• lightweight

Stabilizers

Type	Brand	Description
Tear-Away	• Lightweight Tear-Away (OESD) • Soft Touch Tear-Away (OESD) • Smooth Touch Tear-Away (OESD) • Ultra Clean and Tear (OESD) • Medium Weight Tear-Away (OESD) • Hydro-Stick Tear-Away (OESD) • Stabil-Stick Tear-Away (OESD) • Totally Stable™ (Sulky) • Tear-Easy™ (Sulky) • Stiffy™ (Sulky) • Stitch-n-Tear™ (Pellon)	• non-woven product, similar to paper in that it tears easily • very stable; does not stretch • multiple layers may be used to create greater stability • removed by gently tearing away from stitches • used mainly for woven fabrics • available in many weights, very lightweight to heavy • available in black and white
Cut-Away	• Heavyweight Cut-Away (OESD) • Xtra Heavyweight Cut-Away (OESD) • Hydro-Stick Cut-Away (OESD) • Stabil-Stick Cut-Away (OESD) • Poly Mesh Cut-Away (OESD) • Fusible Poly Mesh Cut-Away (OESD) • Cut-Away Soft 'n Sheer™ (Sulky) • Cut-Away Plus™ (Sulky) • Sof-Stitch™ (Pellon)	• non-woven product that does not tear • provides stability for stitches throughout life of garment/project • very stable; does not stretch • multiple layers may be used to create greater stability • removed by trimming away excess, ¼" from stitches • used mainly for fabrics that stretch • available in many weights, from light to heavy • available in black, white, beige (Poly Mesh)
Water-Soluble	• Aqua Film Topping (OESD) • Aqua Film Backing (OESD) • Aqua Mesh (OESD) • Badge Master (OESD) • Aquabond (QRI) • Wash-A-Way Paper (YLI) • Dissolve 4X (Superior) • Solvy™ (Sulky) • Super Solvy™ (Sulky) • Avalon (Madeira) • Sol-u-Web™ (Pellon) • Tear-n-Wash™ (Pellon)	• usually a clear film • multiple layers may be used to create greater stability • removed by rinsing; leaves no residue • available in many weights, from very light to heavy • lightweight types frequently used as a topping to prevent stitches from sinking into nap of fabric • heavyweight generally used as a backing
Heat-Away	• Heat-Away™ (Sulky)	• disintegrates upon application of heat (pressing) • leaves no fibrous residue • especially good for delicate items that cannot be wet • multiple layers may be used to create greater stability • removed by pressing; chars and turns black, "ash" is easily brushed away
"Sticky Paper"	• Sticky™ (Sulky)	• not a real stabilizer, as may allow fabric to stretch • stable substitute: any stabilizer + adhesive spray, or use OESD Stabil-Stick Cut-Away or Tear-Away stabilizer
Adhesive Sprays	• 202 (temp; paper/fabric) • 404 (perm, repositionable) • 505 (temp; fabric/fabric) • 606 (fusible) • KK 2000 (Sulky) (temp; fabric/fabric) • Quilt Basting Spray (Collins) • Sew Stable (Helmar)	• used to turn any stabilizer into a "sticky" stabilizer • available in temporary and permanent varieties
Starch & Other Fabric Stiffeners	• Perfect Sew (Palmer/Pletsch) • Spray Fabric Stabilizer (Sullivan's) • Sew Stable (Helmar)	• available in spray and paint-on varieties • acts as sizing to provide "crispness" and body to fabric • temporary; removed by washing
Interfacing	• Perfect Fuse (Palmer/Pletsch) • Armo Weft	• available in woven, knit, and non-woven varieties • multiple layers may be used to create greater stability • permanent part of garment/project • used to provide stability to parts of a garment or project; typically collars, cuffs, lapels, plackets, belts, etc. • most varieties allow some stretching of fabric • available in many weights, from very lightweight to heavy • available in white, black, tan, gray, occasionally other colors
Paper	• Stitch & Ditch (8" & 21" wide rolls) • Stitch & Ditch Heirloom (3" wide)	• similar to tear-away stabilizer, but paper-based • embroidery & decorative stitching on very delicate fabrics • useful for heirloom sewing techniques

chapter 5

Although all of the tassels in the Tassels & Trims embroidery collections

have a similar appearance, a variety of digitizing techniques have been

used to create them.

Tassel Embroidery

Becoming familiar with each type of tassel design will help you when selecting specific designs to add to your projects. Some were digitized with one layer of long satin stitches forming the tassels; others have two to three layers for a more definite or heavier look and still others have very short stitches, creating tufts or mini-fringe.

Pay close attention to the clipping instructions, as this is often the step that gives shape and style to each tassel. There are several options for clipping the needle or bobbin threads, each creating a different look. Once the tassels are clipped, they add a three dimensional accent to any embroidered project. Use contrasting bobbin thread when sewing the tassels to make it easy to distinguish the bobbin thread from the needle thread. This simplifies the clipping task and helps ensure that the correct threads are clipped. Once the stitching is completed, the fabric should

be removed from the embroidery hoop before clipping the threads and releasing the tassels.

Along with the digitizing method and clipping technique, another variable that can change the appearance and affect the success of your tassels is your choice of thread. A medium to lightweight thread such as 40 weight rayon gives a lighter, more delicate look to your tassels than a heavier thread such as 30 weight cotton or polyester. For an even heavier trim, use a wool and/or acrylic thread such as Monet by YLI; the thicker fiber creates a bold but cozy appearance.

Once your designs are stitched and clipped to form tassels, use a steam iron to straighten or flatten the hanging threads. Hold the iron above the tassels and steam, using a fine-toothed comb if needed to arrange the threads. Let the tassels dry before moving or disturbing the fabric.

Tassel Styles

Several tassel types were designed and digitized for the Tassels and Trims collections:

Straight Tassel–First, and simplest, is the *basic flat, straight tassel*. These are simply stitched tassels ready to embroider on almost anything, anywhere. After stitching, clip the *needle threads* of these tassels on the back, just below the bobbin threads, then lift the tassel threads carefully to the front and watch this basic trim come alive. Remove any loose and unwanted threads. After steaming and fluffing the tassel, cut all the threads to one length. Leave no looped ends here. This basic tassel adds texture to stitched embroidery designs.

Looped Tassel –A variation on the basic, flat tassel is the *looped tassel*; the loops create a fuller look and add more dimension to larger tassels. When making *looped tassels*, clip or unpick *only the bobbin threads*. Lift the needle threads to the front as for a flat tassel, but *do not trim*. This tassel has a loopy lower edge, creating a fuller tassel. Some flat tassel designs can also be clipped this way; test first, as the success of this variation not only depends on the design of the tassel, but the thread and fabric used as well.

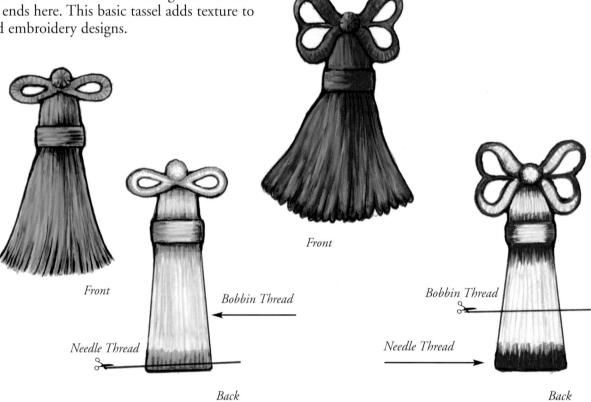

Front

Front

Bobbin Thread

Bobbin Thread

Needle Thread

Needle Thread

Back

Back

Multi-Layered Tassels–Tassels that have been digitized to stitch the hanging portion or "skirt" of the tassels more than once to give a fuller, heavier look to the hanging tassel. The bobbin thread of each layer is clipped separately. When clipping the bobbin thread on the wrong side of the stitching, pay particular attention to avoid clipping the needle threads of the other layers.

Chenille Tassel–A wonderful, three-dimensional detail, this tassel in Collection I is a bit time-consuming, but well worth the effort. It has two rows of vertical satin stitches, reinforced through the center with two rows of running stitches. After stitching the three tassel layers, clip the chenille detail at the top as follows:

Clip chenille stitches only from the right side of the tassel.

Clip the chenille stitches only at the top, and then at the bottom of the two rows.

Using the tip of a pair of small, sharp scissors, lift only the chenille stitches, pulling them taut, away from the center; clip only the outer ends. Do not cut the straight stitches in the center – these stitches secure the chenille embroidery on both sides. Take care not to damage the embroidery underneath the chenille stitches. Do not remove any bobbin threads at this stage. Repeat for the second chenille section.

The lower edge of the tassel should be clipped as desired for a straight or looped tassel.

Chenille and Multi-Layered Tassel Uncut

Chenille and Multi-Layered Tassel Cut

When all embroidery is complete, steam-press the tassels and chenille details, holding the iron close to the embroidery for a few seconds before taking it away. This will be sufficient for lifting the chenille details. Let cool.

Tufts–Tiny tassels that are normally grouped together as part of an embroidery design. As these tassels are very small, *only the bobbin threads* are cut or removed, otherwise the tassels would be too short. *Do not cut the*

needle threads. Tufts are usually stitched in one color to ensure the desired effect.

Fringe–Formed by long satin stitches, fringe is often used to accentuate the center of a flower. Only when the fringe is cut does the flower "bloom". When stitching fringed flowers, add an extra layer of stabilizer underneath the hoop before stitching the long satin stitches. This provides a shield for the previous stitching and helps prevent damaging the embroidery underneath the fringe when the threads are cut. Clip the bobbin thread of the long satin stitches

Fringe Uncut

Fringe Cut

from the wrong side of the design. From the front, fluff the needle thread, releasing it to form the fringe.

Multi-Tiered Tassels–Large designs with overlapping rows or tiers of basic tassels, these tassels are often stitched in different colors to emphasize and/or differentiate the layers. These tassels are stitched, clipped, and trimmed the same way as single tassels and are wonderful for projects requiring a prominent or heavy border or hem.

Multi-Tiered Tassels Uncut

Multi-Tiered Tassels Cut

Trims that coordinate with the tassel designs offer unlimited creative possibilities when using the three Tassels & Trims embroidery collections.

Embroidered Trims & Edge Finishes

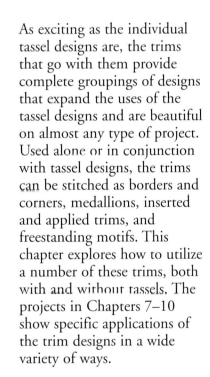

As exciting as the individual tassel designs are, the trims that go with them provide complete groupings of designs that expand the uses of the tassel designs and are beautiful on almost any type of project. Used alone or in conjunction with tassel designs, the trims can be stitched as borders and corners, medallions, inserted and applied trims, and freestanding motifs. This chapter explores how to utilize a number of these trims, both with and without tassels. The projects in Chapters 7–10 show specific applications of the trim designs in a wide variety of ways.

The appendices in the back of the book show all of the designs included in the three *Tassels & Trims* collections. Most of the motifs were created as individual elements of matched groupings, and all can be used singly or with other coordinating components. This is a great way to select designs for related items such as a tablecloth and a topper (see Tabletop Ballerina in Chapter 7) or a pillowcase and sheets (see Butterfly Bed Linens in Chapter 8) or even a cardigan and pullover top (see Tasseled Twin Set in Chapter 8). By using a border design and a coordinating single motif scattered across the fabric (see Sheer Christening Dress in Chapter 9), you can bring harmony to almost any project. Or, by combining the related elements within a group (see Tufted Tablecloth in Chapter 7) you can create a balanced design to scatter across the fabric of your next project.

On the following pages, some uses of these trims are detailed, showing how to stitch and use them for different applications such as at corners, on curved edges, as baby trims, and as shaped borders. As you experiment, feel free to rearrange and regroup the designs as you wish. Mix and match the trims with any of the tassel designs. Even though they were designed as coordinated groups, many of them will mesh with designs from other groupings for exciting looks.

Continuous Borders

Many of the design elements can be linked together to form continuous borders placed completely on the fabric or applied along a shaped edge to form the outer edge of a project. Both start the same way. Note that your fabric may have to be re-hooped to stitch a border long enough for your project.

Examples of continuous borders can be seen in the Trimmed Capri Pants in Chapter 7, on the skirt of the Sheer Christening Dress and along the hem of the Bordered Curtain, both in Chapter 9.

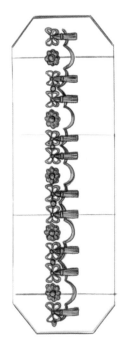

Use your embroidery software or the on-screen editing capabilities of your embroidery system to link the desired motifs and form a continuous border:

Select the desired motif; position vertically within the hoop outline.

Duplicate the motif; align with previous motif, overlapping slightly. Use the grid function to aid in aligning designs.

Continue duplicating and aligning motifs until hoop is full.

Decide where the border will be stitched. Stitch a basting line at the decided position, taking into account any hem allowances, or draw a line with a fabric marker. If embroidering a shaped border, place the line about 1"–2" above the edge of the fabric, making sure the linked motifs will be stitched completely on the fabric (the excess will be trimmed away later). *Note: This line will be used to center the linked motifs each time the fabric is hooped.*

Stabilize the fabric appropriately and hoop the stabilized fabric, placing the marked or basted line in the center of the hoop.

Attach the hoop to the machine. Align the center of the linked designs with the marked or basted line on the fabric.

Stitch the linked designs, changing thread colors as desired. Continue until all the designs within the hoop are completely embroidered.

Remove the hoop from the machine and the fabric from the hoop.

Stabilize and re-hoop the fabric, positioning the hoop so that the next stitching is aligned with the previously stitched designs. Check to make sure the second hooping is in the correct position by aligning the center of the linked designs to the drawn or basted line.

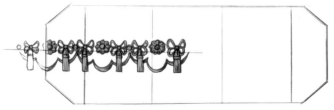

Stitch the second hooping, changing thread colors as desired. Continue re-hooping and stitching until the desired area is covered with the border.

When the stitching is complete, remove the hoop from the machine and the fabric from the hoop. Gently remove excess stabilizer and trim loose threads.

To use the stitched border as a shaped edge, trim the excess fabric away from the outer edge of the stitched designs. Apply seam sealant to the cut edge after trimming is complete.

Applied Trims

Some linked motifs lend themselves to being stitched as "yardage" and used in the same ways as purchased trims: inserted into seams, applied over raw fabric edges or attached to finished edges. Examples of applied trims can be seen on the upper edge for the Ballerina Lamp Shade in Chapter 7 and as a border trim on the Embroidered Holiday Candle in Chapter 8.

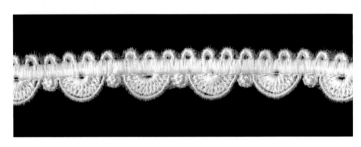

To create these trims, begin in the same manner as for continuous borders. Use your embroidery software or the on-screen editing capabilities of your embroidery system to link the desired motifs to form a continuous length of trim.

Select the desired motif; position vertically within the hoop outline.

Duplicate the motif; align with previous motif, overlapping slightly. Use the grid function to aid in aligning designs. Continue duplicating and aligning motifs until hoop is full.

Thread the embroidery machine using the same thread type and color in both the bobbin and the needle.

Hoop 2–3 layers of a water-soluble stabilizer such as Aqua Film (or 1 layer of Badgemaster).

Stitch until the linked designs in the hoop are completely embroidered, changing thread colors as desired.

Note: To make longer lengths of trim, rehoop and stitch the linked designs again, aligning the second hooping with the first to make a continuous line of trim. Continue rehooping and stitching until the desired length of trim is stitched.

When the stitching is complete, remove the hoop from the machine and the fabric from the hoop. Completely remove stabilizer and trim loose threads. Use the trim as you would use a purchased edging.

Freestanding Motifs

Often used to add dimension to an embroidered project, freestanding motifs are stitched on water-soluble stabilizer in the same manner as applied trims.

Hoop 2–3 layers of a water-soluble stabilizer such as Aqua Film (or 1 layer of Badgemaster).

Stitch the desired design until completely embroidered, changing thread colors as desired.

Note: Designs selected for this type of embellishment must have enough structure to hold together once the stabilizer is removed. If they do not, stitch them on polyester organdy or tulle and use a heat tool (such as a stencil burner) to remove the excess fabric from around the design after the stitching is complete. Protect your work surface with glass or ceramic tile and ALWAYS do a test design first.

When the stitching is complete, remove the hoop from the machine and the fabric from the hoop. Completely remove stabilizer and trim loose threads.

Attach the freestanding motifs to your project by tacking them in place for a 3-dimensional effect or by appliquéing around the edges for a flat look.

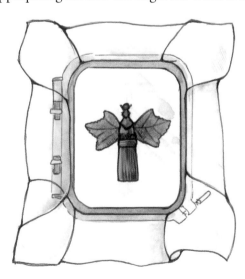

Shaped Trims

Only narrow trims can be "forced" into new shapes by molding them with steam while still warm. The "mock crochet trim" of Collection I (Motif #20) was used on the top, curved edge of the Ballerina Lampshade in Chapter 7. This method was used as straight trims cannot be stitched around a curved edge.

Note: Designs selected for this type of embellishment must have enough structure to hold together once the stabilizer is removed. If they do not, stitch them on polyester organdy or tulle and use a heat tool (such as a stencil burner) to remove the excess fabric from around the design after the stitching is complete.

To create a narrow trim, begin in the same manner as for continuous borders. Use your embroidery software or the on-screen editing capabilities of your embroidery system to link the desired motifs to form a continuous length of trim.

Select the desired motif; position vertically within the hoop outline.

Duplicate the motif; align with previous motif, overlapping slightly. Use the grid function to aid in aligning designs. Continue duplicating and aligning motifs until hoop is full or until you have the required length for your project.

Embroider the trim on a layer of organza (the same color as the trim) hooped with a layer of water-soluble stabilizer.

When embroidery is complete, remove the fabric from the hoop and rinse in water until all the stabilizer is removed.

Carefully trim the excess fabric from the top and bottom edges. Do not damage any of the surrounding satin stitches.

Trace the curved edge needed for the project—e.g. lamp shade edge—on a blank piece of white paper and use this as a guide/template for "shaping" the trim. Pin this guide to the ironing board.

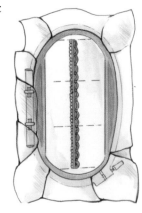

Lay the trim flat on the template, wrong side facing up. Adjust the steam iron settings as recommended for the project fabric (see iron manufacturers instructions).

Starting at one end, use a little steam to shape the trim as needed. *TIP: Steam one section at a time, then —while the trim is still warm— gently push the upper edge and stretch the lower edge to form the required curves.*

Let trim cool completely before lifting it from the ironing board.

Glue or hand-sew the newly shaped trim to the finished project. To finish, fold in and trim the ends where they meet.

Appliquéd Trims

Some motifs have been digitized as appliqué designs and provide a way to add fabric accents to a border or strip of continuous trim. Designs #47, #52, #53, and #54 of Collection I can be stitched as appliquéd trims using the following directions:

To create an appliquéd trim, begin in the same manner as for continuous borders. Use your embroidery software or the on-screen editing capabilities of your embroidery system to link the desired motifs to form a length of continuous trim.

Select the desired motif; position vertically within the hoop outline.

Duplicate the motif; align with previous motif, overlapping slightly. Use the grid function to aid in aligning designs. Continue duplicating and aligning motifs until hoop is full or until you have the required length for your project.

When the machine stops after the first stage, place a long strip of appliqué fabric over the stitched area, placing one end of the appliqué strip at the beginning of the embroidery. *Note: The appliqué strip must be the same length as the completed border. To keep the strip in place, spray the wrong side with temporary spray adhesive. Smooth appliqué strip in place.*

Stitch the next portion of the motif.

Remove the hoop from the machine. Do not remove the fabric from the hoop. Cut *only* the appliqué fabric from the top and bottom edges of the trim. Do *not* cut the appliqué fabric at the ends (sides) where the next motifs will be linked and stitched. Keep in mind where the top and bottom edges are if the trims have been rotated and placed vertically in the hoop.

Replace the hoop in the machine and continue stitching until the first motif is embroidered successfully.

Rehoop the fabric as necessary, repeating the above steps until the appliqué border is complete.

Remove the fabric from the hoop. Remove stabilizer and unwanted loose threads.

If stitched as part of a project, cut excess fabric from around the scallops only.

To use as a separate trim, cut the fabric at the top satin edge away. Use the completed strip as a "free-standing" border. Attach to a finished projects such as curtains or ready-made linens along the top satin stitches.

Medallions

Many of the designs in the collections can be used not just as single motifs, but combined to create larger medallions. These are best used on large, open areas or the effect might be too extravagant. The medallion used on the Pretty Posies Tea Tray in Chapter 9 is an example of how striking a group of designs can be when arranged in a geometric—circular, rectangular, diamond-shaped, or hexagonal— arrangement. Stitched tone-on-tone, medallions have the same effect as embossed designs on curtains and other projects. Add a hint of metallic thread and you have created your own unique fabric.

To stitch a medallion design, simply use your embroidery software or the on-screen editing capabilities of your embroidery system to position several motifs in a circular arrangement. Stabilize your fabric appropriately and hoop the stabilized fabric. Stitch the arranged motifs as one design, changing thread colors and rehooping as desired.

Eyelet Trims and Cutwork Designs

Embroidered eyelets and cutwork designs add a rich look when included as parts of stitched designs. Fashionable when used as part of a "lace-up" project, these types of designs can be combined with other designs for decorative purposes.

The unique eyelet top shown here and the Renaissance Belt in Chapter 9 show practical ways to use both eyelet trims and cutwork motifs.

On the eyelet top, the eyelet trims were stitched in the same manner as applied trims. After the stabilizer was removed, the trims were used on the lower edge of the top and the upper edge of the peplum. After the centers of the eyelets were punched out, the bodice and peplum of the blouse were joined by lacing a thin gold cord through the eyelets. The same technique was used to join the lower sleeve edges to the flounces that finish them. Designed as Mega Hoop designs, lengths of eyelets can easily be stitched on several garment sections in just a few hoopings; for instance, the eyelets on the lower bodice edge and the eyelet trim with tassels on the lower scallops can be stitched in one hooping.

Other uses for embroidered eyelets include center front closures, joining skirt sections, pants sides seams, joining vertical sleeve sections, pillow and cushion covers—the possibilities are endless.

The links of the belt are actually complete, freestanding cutwork motifs, laced together to form a belt. In this case, the edges are reinforced with brass grommets and the belt is laced with leather cording.

chapter 7

The beautiful tassels and textured trims in Collection I were just the beginning of creative inspiration using these feminine motifs.

Projects: Collection I

The designs that started it all are just as exciting today as when they were introduced by BERNINA® of America. Collection I has several groupings of designs that lend themselves to the creation of tasseled edgings, "crochet-look" trims, and feminine motifs. Using the individual motifs and grouping them in different ways lets you coordinate several items without stitching the exact same design on each. Motifs can be combined and arranged using embroidery software or the on-screen editing features of your embroidery machine.

This chapter has several projects including a delightful group for creating a display table any young girl would love! The embroidered lampshade, round tablecloth and double-layer topper all coordinate to give a beautiful look to an

occasional table for the bedroom or sitting area.

An embroidery motif stitched along the hem of purchased Capri pants offers a way to give a finished look to any project. The short tassels extend beyond the finished hem for a fun look and feel to otherwise "plain" jeans.

Another tablecloth uses a group of tufted designs to add interest to the outer edges, leaving the center open for tabletop accessories.

In addition to the designs used for these projects, this collection includes several styles of individual tassels, groupings that offer corner options, several border designs, butterflies, scallops, and heart motifs. For a look at the entire collection, see Appendix A on page 91 of this book.

- Pattern Ease by HTC
- Fabric marker
- Firmly woven fabric–amount determined by size of pattern (see below)
- Matching polyester organza
- Tear-Away stabilizer
- Temporary fabric adhesive such as 505 spray
- Isacord embroidery thread in desired color
- Fabric glue
- Aqua Film stabilizer
- Sharp trimming scissors
- Seam sealant such Fray Stoppa by Helmar

Preparation

Create a pattern for the lampshade by laying it on its side on a large piece of Pattern Ease. Align the seam of the shade with one of the edges of the Pattern Ease. Roll the shade and mark along the top and bottom until you reach the seam. Add about 1/2" (1.2cm) to each straight edge for seam allowances. You should have a semi-circular pattern; cut out the pattern.

Mark the pattern into five equal sections as shown. Draw two lines 3 1/2" (8.9cm) and 1" (2.5cm) from the outer circular edge. These will be the placement lines for the hearts and the "border" motifs. Using a fabric marker, transfer pattern and markings to fabric.

Tabletop Ballerina: Lampshade, Tablecloth and Topper

A little girl's fantasy come true! A coordinating tablecloth and lampshade over a glass ballerina lamp base. Using your favorite novelty lamp base, make this coordinating table set and create a unique display area. See photos on pages 28 and 118.

Lampshade

Create a custom look for any decor by embroidering fabric to coordinate with other items in the room. The following directions are general in nature for a "cone-shaped" lampshade. Adjust them as needed to accommodate your shade.

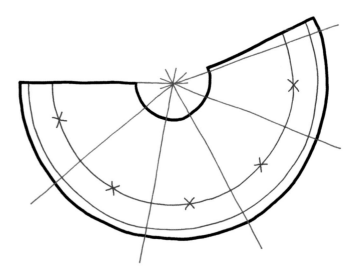

Embroidery

Using temporary fabric adhesive spray, bond organza to the right side of the fabric in the areas where the hearts will be embroidered. Stabilize the fabric and hoop the stabilized fabric; place hoop on machine.

Embroider the heart motif #19/16/11 without the side circles, centering the designs between the straight lines. Rehoop and stitch the motif in each section, treating as an appliqué, trimming away fabric and stabilizer as needed.

Embroider the scallop motif #22/19/14 on the 1" (2.5cm) marked line, centering each one under each heart. Stitch motif #21/18/13 on organza, rehooping as needed. Determine the number of units needed to fill the spaces between the scallops, then embroider all units in one hooping. Stitch only the tiny picot edging at the top of the motif; omit the rest of the design, forwarding the sewing sequence to finish with the satin stitching, forming a narrow strip to complete the lower edge. Trim excess fabric from the upper and lower edges. Put seam sealant on the cut edges.

Covering the Shade

Wrap the embroidered fabric around the shade, positioning the lower edge as desired and overlapping cut edges. Mark the seamline; also mark the placement of the hearts on the shade.

Remove the fabric and stitch to form a circle, seaming on the marked lines. Cut the heart shapes from the lampshade.

Place the fabric on the shade, positioning the heart designs over the cut-out heart shapes. Trim the upper edge of the fabric even with the upper edge of the shade. Glue the fabric in place along the upper edge.

Trim the lower edge of the fabric around the scallops. Snip into the sides of each side circle on scallops; center and glue the narrow trims between the scallops, pressing the trim edges between the snipped edges of the circles.

Upper Trim

Hoop 1–2 layers of Aqua Film stabilizer and embroider motif #20/17/12 linking enough sections to trim the upper edge of the shade. Remove the stabilizer and using your steam iron, shape the trim into a curve as directed in Chapter 6 and glue in place over the upper raw fabric edge.

Circular Tablecloth & Square Fringed Topper

This circular tablecloth and its unique double-layer topper are made of the same fabric, embroidered with the same motifs as the lampshade for a completely coordinated look.

Supplies

- 4 yards (3.66m) of 54" (137cm) wide fabric
- 1 yard matching polyester organza
- Matching construction thread
- 3 cones matching serger thread
- Matching embroidery thread
- Water-soluble stabilizer such as Aqua Mesh
- Universal needles–Size #70/10
- Embroidery needles–Size #75/11
- Water-soluble marking pen
- Fabric glue
- Edgestitch foot (BERNINA® Foot #10/10C)
- Open embroidery foot (BERNINA® Foot #20/20C)
- Serger

Preparation

Pre-wash and press fabric before cutting.

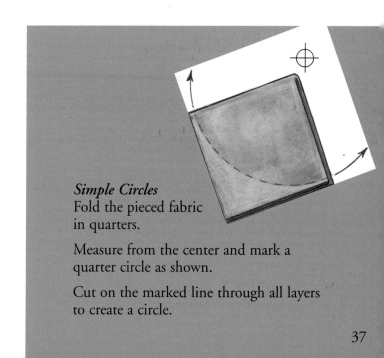

Simple Circles

Fold the pieced fabric in quarters.

Measure from the center and mark a quarter circle as shown.

Cut on the marked line through all layers to create a circle.

Circular Tablecloth

Cut a 76" (193cm) length of fabric (54" (137cm) wide); remaining fabric should be a 72" (183cm) length (54" (137cm) wide). Cut a 25" (63.5cm) strip from the 72" x 54" (183cm x 137cm) rectangle. Seam to 76" x 54" (193cm x 137cm) rectangle as shown. Cut a 75" (190.5cm) diameter circle from the pieced fabric (see page 37).

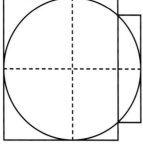

Fold circle in quarters. Mark fold lines with creases by pressing lightly.

Set serger for a narrow 3-thread overlock. Adjust differential to 0.7; this will cause the stitching to gather slightly. Serge around outer edge of circle, barely trimming the edge. Press serged edge to wrong side, forming a narrow hem.

Set sewing machine for a straight stitch using matching thread. Attach an edgestitch foot to the machine; set needle position to the far left. Using the guide of the foot, topstitch the hem in place.

At each marked quarter line, mark a point 5½" (14cm) from the hemmed edge; these mark the centers of the hearts (design #19/16/11).

Using temporary adhesive spray, bond a piece of organza under the embroidery area. Adhere Aqua Film stabilizer to the back of the tablecloth. Using embroidery thread to match the fabric, stitch the first color of the heart motif; a straight stitch outline will be sewn.

Carefully remove the embroidery hoop from the machine. Do NOT unhoop the fabric! Carefully trim away the solid fabric from inside the outline; do not cut the organza or stabilizer.

Re-attach hoop to machine; continue embroidering. When all four hearts have been stitched, trim excess organza from the wrong side and remove stabilizer.

Topper

Cut a 28" x 28" (71.2cm x 71.2cm) square of solid fabric and a 26" x 26" (66cm x 66cm) square of sheer fabric.

Thread sewing machine with matching embroidery thread. Stitch around entire outside edge of the 28" x 28" (71.2cm x 71.2cm) square of solid fabric, 1" (2.5cm) in from the edge, using an overcast, blindstitch, or blanket stitch that "points in" to the center of the cloth. *Tip: If using a BERNINA® machine, attach the right side Seam Guide with Ruler to the back of the foot; adjust the guide to 1" (2.5cm) from the center needle position. Stitch with the seam guide positioned along the raw edge of the fabric, pivoting at the corners.*

Fringe the outer edges of the fabric square.

Draw a 22" x 22" (55.9cm x 55.9cm) square in the center of the organza and mark a line 1" (2.5cm) inside the edges of the square.

Stabilize and hoop one corner of the organza. Stitch design #20/17/12 along each side of the hooped corner. Stitch round design #21/16/11 over the point of the corner. Trim on drawn line.

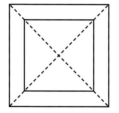

Fold each fabric square in half diagonally; mark diagonals. Place embroidered square on plain square; use marked diagonals to center the small square on the large one.

Thread sewing machine with embroidery thread; select straight stitch. Straight stitch 1" (2.5cm) in from each edge of the sheer fabric, connecting the embroidered corners. Fringe all four sides of the sheer square. Select satin stitch; sew over straight stitching.

Tufted Tablecloth

This simple linen cloth, shown on page 34, is embellished with a tufted design stitched with subtle colors in the same color family as the fabric. The stitched embroidery designs form a large square, set on-point, leaving the center of the cloth open for placing a tea service, bedside lamp, or other item on the tabletop (see page 34). A coordinating motif is scattered around the outer edges of the embroidered square and the edges of the cloth are fringed for a finishing touch.

Supplies

- 1 1/8 yards (1.03m) of heavyweight cotton or linen (prewash & press)
- Isacord embroidery thread in desired colors
- Yenmet metallic embroidery thread
- Bobbin thread to match fabric
- Tear-Away stabilizer
- Temporary fabric adhesive such as 505 spray
- Embroidery needles–Size #75/11
- Metallica or Metafil needles–Size #80/12
- Water-soluble marking pen
- Open embroidery foot (BERNINA® Foot #20/20C)

Preparation

Pre-wash and press fabric. Fold in half and lightly press a crease down the center, then fold it again across the center and press a second crease to divide the cloth into four equal quarters.

Using water-soluble marking pen and the quarter pattern for the Tufted Tablecloth, transfer the markings onto the linen fabric, rotating the pattern sheet and transferring all the markings to all four quarters.

Embroidery

Using embroidery software or the on-screen editing features of your

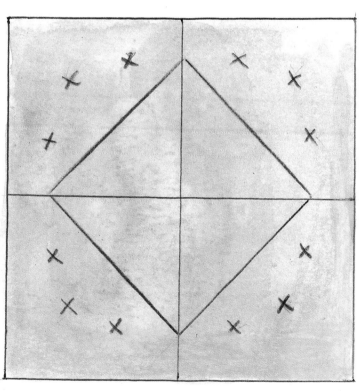

embroidery machine, combine design #69/62/56 and #67/60/54 to create the following combination.

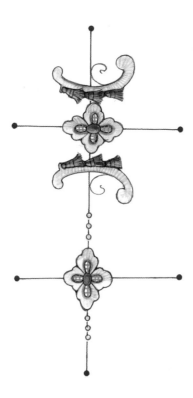

Fill spaces between motifs with small flower design #69/62/56, or edit the motifs in the software by adding three "French knots" or candlewicking stitches.

Using temporary adhesive spray, adhere 1–2 layers of stabilizer under the embroidery area. Using the desired embroidery thread colors, stitch the motifs, using metallic thread in the center of the flower motif. Rehoop as needed to stitch all four sides of the embroidered square and the scattered motifs.

When the embroidery is complete, remove the hoop from the machine and the fabric from the hoop. Gently tear away all stabilizer.

Fringing/Finishing

Attach an open embroidery foot to the sewing machine. Select the blanket stitch; if needed, engage Mirror Image so that the stitches "point" to the left, away from the raw edge. Thread needle and bobbin with embroidery or construction thread to match fabric. Stitch around all four sides of the rectangle, 1" (2.5cm) from the edge, pivoting at the corners.

Tip: If using a BERNINA® machine, attach the right side Seam Guide with Ruler to the back of the foot; adjust the guide to 1" (2.5cm) from the center needle position. Stitch with the seam guide positioned along the raw edge of the fabric, pivoting at the corners.

Carefully remove fabric yarns from outer edge of the cloth (outside of the blanket stitching) to create fringe around all four sides.

Trimmed Capri Pants

Dress up a purchased pair of jeans or an old pair of trousers by adding embroidery to the hem. Choose a motif with free-hanging tassels, such as motif #37/30/24 from *Tassels & Trims I.*

Supplies
- Ready-made jeans or trousers
- Adhesive stabilizer such as Stabil-Stick
- Embroidery thread, including gold metallic thread for tassels
- Seam sealant, such as *Fray Stoppa* by Helmar
- Hand sewing needle

Directions
Open the inside leg seams by removing the overlock stitching as far as possible. If the hem is very bulky, remove the stitching and re-hem the pants after the embroidery is completed.

Adhere adhesive stabilizer to the bottom of the embroidery hoop and attach the hoop to the machine.

Smooth the lower edge of one pant leg onto the stabilizer.

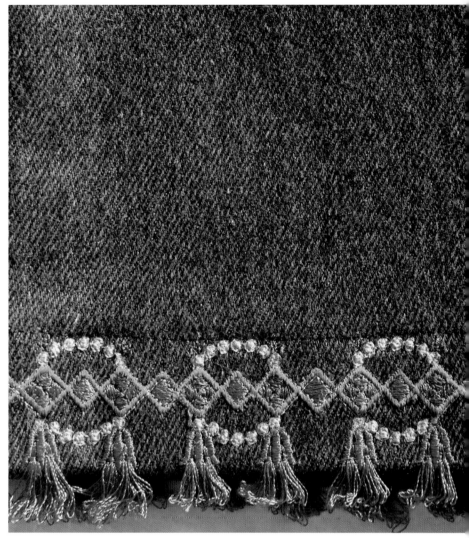

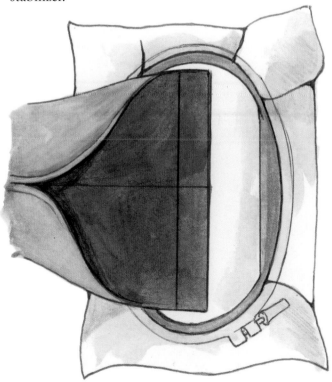

Embroider the tassel border along the hemline, rehooping and/or repositioning as needed.

When the embroidery is complete, remove all of the stabilizer and trim away all loose threads. Clip the bobbin thread of each tassel. Gently pull the tassels loose from the fabric; trim the lower edge of the tassels.

With right sides together, re-stitch and/or overlock the inside leg seams. Neaten the seam where the new embroidered seam and hem meet. Re-hem the pants if needed, carefully avoiding the free hanging tassels. The tassels should extend slightly below the lower edge of the pants.

This collection of distinctive designs offer luxury and grace to all of your projects. For a look at all of the designs in Collection II, see Appendix B on page 99.

Projects: Collection II

The elegance and beauty of *Tassels & Trims* continues with Collection II, which offers beautiful tasseled borders— both single and multi-tiered, simple corner motifs, and unique eyelet trims. The projects detailed in the following pages are embellished with motifs from Collection II and offer a variety of looks from the richly elegant Quilted Cushion to the beaded sophistication of the Tasseled Twin Set.

The Quilted Tassel Cushion is an example of the dramatic effect that repeating a single motif can produce. If practice makes perfect, you'll be an expert at stitching and clipping tassels by the time you finish this project.

The Tasseled Throw is one of the most striking, yet simple, projects in this book: a rectangle of gorgeous fabric with a continuous border of free hanging tassels on two

edges and a simple turned and stitched hem on the other two sides. Using a heavy acrylic thread and fringing the fabric under the tasseled edges adds to the richness of the tassels and provides a finishing touch for this cozy project.

The unique table topper shown on page 50 starts with four quarter-circles of fabric, joined with decorative openwork fagoting—hand-look stitching worked on the sewing machine—to make a circle. It is then embellished with sheer appliqué techniques and a scalloped border which transform this plain linen circle into the elegant Overlay Appliqué Topper.

For custom embroidered bed linens, dress up a purchased sheet and pillowcase with a contrasting border and sweet butterfly and forget-me-not motifs. The butterfly design is perfect for that special little girl who is growing up so fast; change the color scheme and it becomes a sophisticated sheet ensemble appropriate for adults. Combine components of this grouping to create a border, linking smaller elements to Mega Hoop motif #46 on the edge of a top sheet. Scatter tiny flower bouquets or flower ringlets, motifs #42–44/38–40/37–49, on her pillowcase and, to top it all, embroider the single tassel butterfly on her pajamas! Don't forget to embroider the large butterfly on her bath towel.

Use other elements from the diverse assortment of embroidered trims and tassels in this collection to create a holiday centerpiece by attaching embroidered motifs to a candle and to add a unique touch to a cardigan and shell for an elegant, tasseled twin set.

Along with the designs featured on the projects in this chapter, the *Tassels & Trims II* embroidery collection offers a wide array of imaginative trims for use in future projects (see Appendix B for design images).

Daisy Heirloon–motifs #22–28/22–27/22–27: A selection of dainty flowers combined with delicate scallops, bows, and tassels, these single color motifs can be linked and combined to create a continuous border—perfect for that curtain that needs a face lift—or used singly to create an all-over pattern. Using the Mega Hoop and motif #28—the equivalent of six single motifs—allows long borders to be embroidered on a project in a jiffy. For shorter borders, combine multiples of motif #26. Motif #25—a complete single unit—offers additional creative options for customizing bed linens, tablecloths, and curtains. Link single flowers #27 and tassels #22 with scallop #23 for a variation.

Hidden Hearts–motifs #51–57/45–50/42–46: Link these medieval-looking motifs to expose the hearts that are formed when the scrolls at the sides are joined. Combine to create lacy borders, corner motifs, or mix coordinating motifs for a variety of effects.

Eyelet Trim–motifs #63–70/55–59/51–55: Elaborate, monochrome scallops, tasseled bows and eyelets make up this unique set of trims. Create a continuous border by linking multiples of scallop and eyelet motif #65/57/53, or use the Mega Hoop design #68—the equivalent of four #65s—along one edge of a project. Repeat just the line of eyelets (#68/59/55 or Mega Hoop #70) in the same length for the opposite side. Trim the fabric from around the eyelets and use an awl to punch out the centers of both lengths of eyelets. Trim the fabric from around the scallops and lace the two edges together with a narrow ribbon or a satin cord. Use this technique to attach the lower section of a blouse to the upper bodice, and lower sleeves to upper sleeves. Add a scallop frill or border to an upper curtain using the same eyelet motifs. Endless possibilities!

Quilted Tassel Cushion

A dramatic, heavily embroidered cushion for that special spot still to be filled in your lounge or bedroom. For this exquisite cushion use a heavy, richly textured fabric and keep adding tassels, scattering them over the quilting.

Supplies

- 1½ yards x 45" (1.5m x 1.15m wide) good quality two tone fabric such as Crushed Shimmer Organza
- 17¼" (45cm) invisible zipper
- Two contrasting or coordinating embroidery threads as desired–in this case black Isacord and metallic gold such as Yenmet
- Bobbin thread–same thread as embroidery thread used to embroider tassels
- Construction thread compatible to the fabric
- 25" x 25" (50cm x 50cm) batting such as Warm 'N Natural for quilting
- 1½ yards x 45" (1.50m x 1.15m) black polyester/cotton–18" x 18" (50cm x 50cm) for backing of quilting
- 20" (51cm) square pillow form
- 2½ yards (2m) heavy, corded trim with flange
- BERNINA® *Tassels & Trims II* embroidery collection CD
- BERNINA® *artista* 200E
- Mega Hoop or largest hoop available for your embroidery module/machine
- Medium Hoop (for adding smaller tassels over the quilting)
- Embroidery Wand (optional)
- Overlock foot (BERNINA® #2/2A)
- Invisible zipper foot (BERNINA® #35)
- Walking foot (BERNINA® #50)
- Zipper foot for attaching corded trim (BERNINA® #4)
- Embroidery needle #75/11
- Metallica needle #80/12
- Universal needle #80/12 or #75/11
- Tracing wheel & paper
- Clear ruler–24" long
- Straight pins
- Temporary adhesive such as 505 spray
- Scissors (for cutting)
- Small sharp scissors for cutting tassels
- Stabilizer such as Lightweight Tear-Away or Stitch & Tear–2 layers

Preparation

Trace and transfer the topper pattern, all the quilting lines, seams and embroidery lines onto the fabric. Leave a wide strip of fabric 3"–4" (8–10cm) beyond the outer cutting line to allow for easy hooping. This excess fabric will be trimmed away once the embroidery and quilting are complete.

Using the template for motif #101 (*Tassels & Trims II* CD), transfer all placement lines and centers onto the fabric.

Fill at least two bobbins with black bobbin thread.

Embroidery

Adhere two layers of stabilizer to the back of the cushion fabric and hoop fabric. Attach the hoop to the machine and select the trim design. Using the placement arrows, position the design to stitch in the upper left corner of the cushion top. Embroider the design.

When the stitching is complete, remove the hoop from the machine and carefully remove the fabric from the hoop. Remove the stabilizer and clip unwanted threads.

Place black cotton fabric (lining) *right side down* on a flat surface. Place batting on lining, then place embroidered fabric right side up on the batting. "Baste" all layers together using temporary spray adhesive.

Set machine for a straight stitch with length of 3mm–3.5mm; black embroidery thread in the needle, and black bobbin thread. Attach walking foot. Starting at the center and working toward the outer edges, quilt all transferred lines in a grid pattern. *Note: Black machine quilting thread—such as Mettler cotton quilting thread—can be used instead of embroidery thread if desired.*

Change to a Metallica needle and gold metallic thread; loosen the needle tension slightly. Select desired quilting stitch from the list on the following page. Topstitch two outer lines surrounding the quilted blocks, taking care when stitching around the shaped parts of the embroidery. Keep this topstitching on the inside of the satin stitch embroidery.

There are several stitches on the *artista* 200 that are suitable for quilting the cushion:
- #324–straight stitch with securing program–locks stitches at the beginning and end of each seam
- #325–quilting straight stitch–automatically set for a shorter than usual straight stitch
- #328 and #346-350–hand-look quilt stitches in a variety of sizes–used with clear monofilament thread in needle, produces the look of a hand-sewn running stitch

Select single tassel #60/53/47 from the *Tassels & Trims II* collection.

Change back to an Embroidery needle and thread machine with black embroidery thread.

Carefully hoop quilted fabric in the Mega Hoop; no stabilizer is needed. Starting at the left and working around to the right, stitch single tassels at the corners of each diamond (grid intersections) until all tassels in this hoop position have been stitched. Re-hoop as needed until the entire quilted area has been filled with tassels. Tie off all loose ends and trim thread tails.

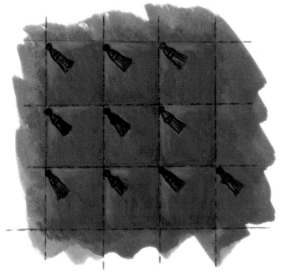

Tip: When stitching the tassels on the thick quilted fabric, the top thread is too short to continue to the next tassel. This slows the process, as the upper thread has to be pulled down by hand and the needle has to be rethreaded. To avoid this on the artista embroidery machine, disable the Auto Thread Cutter (Setup > Embroidery Settings 2) when embroidering the tassels.

On the wrong side of the cushion top, clip the bobbin threads of all of the tassels with small, sharp scissors. Working from the front of the cushion top, use the Embroidery Wand (optional) or the tip of the scissors to carefully loosen and lift tassels. Steam tassels *very lightly* and fluff immediately by hand to straighten tassel ends. Do not flatten

tassels with the steam iron. Trim tassel ends to one length.

Pillow Construction

Using an overlock foot (BERNINA® #2/2A), and an overlock stitch, overcast the raw edges of the center back seam. *Note: Edges can also be finished using a 2- or 3-thread serger overlock stitch.*

Insert a Universal needle, size #70/10; thread machine with construction thread to match cushion. Set machine for a straight stitch; attach an invisible zipper foot (BERNINA® #35). Insert invisible zipper into center back seam following instructions packaged with presser foot.

Trim the quilted cushion front to the exact size as the pattern. Starting in the middle of one side, and using a zipper foot, stitch the corded trim around the outer edge of the cushion front using a 3/4" (1.9cm) seam allowance, tucking ends into seam. *Tip: Unwind the ends of the trim for easier stitching and to ensure a neat, flat finish at the edge of the cushion.*

Place cushion top right sides together on the cushion back; pin in place. *Note: Unzip zipper a few inches so that cushion can be easily turned right side out when complete.* Using a zipper foot, straight stitch around the outer edge of cushion, just inside previous line of stitching. Neaten and trim edges and corners where necessary. Turn cushion right side out and neaten corners.

Insert the pillow form through the zipper opening in the back and close the zipper.

Butterfly Bed Linens

Customize purchased bed linens by adding a contrasting border and a spray of embroidered designs along the hem.

Supplies

- Purchased flat sheet
- Purchased standard pillowcase
- Firmly woven fabric in a contrasting color to the linens
- Isacord embroidery thread
- Poly Mesh stabilizer
- 505 temporary spray adhesive
- Fabric marker
- Open embroidery foot (BERNINA® #20/20C)
- Embroidery needle #75/11
- Universal needle #80/12

Bordered Sheet

Remove the stitching of the hem along the upper edge of the sheet and press.

Measure 6" (15.3cm) down from the upper edge; using a fabric marker, draw a line across the sheet. This line will be the center point of the stitched embroidery designs.

Using spray adhesive, bond Poly Mesh to the wrong side of the sheet, covering the area above and below the drawn line.

Find the center of the upper edge; mark it on the drawn line. Hoop the stabilized sheet, placing the center of the drawn line in the center of the hoop.

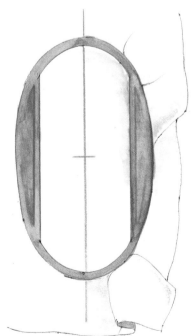

Stitch the butterfly design (#45/41/–) from Collection II in the center of the upper edge of the sheet. Stitch the designs shown below (#43/39/38 and #44/40/39) on each side of the butterfly, rehooping as needed.

Note: If using the Collection II CD and a Mega Hoop, these motifs have already been combined for you in design #46.

After all stitching is complete, remove as much of the stabilizer as possible.

Cut a 7" (17.8cm) strip for the border from the contrasting fabric, making it wide enough to fit across the upper edge of the flat sheet with 1/2" (1.2cm) extending past the finished side edges.

Fold the strip in half across the width to make a strip 3½" (9cm) wide.

Using spray adhesive, "baste" the border to the upper edge of the sheet, folding it over the raw edge of the sheet.

Using the enclosed pattern and a fabric marker, draw the shaped edge of the border as shown.

Straight stitch along the drawn line, stitching through all layers. Using sharp scissors, trim the excess fabric next to the stitching.

Attach an open embroidery foot (BERNINA® #20/20C) and set the machine for satin stitching; satin stitch over the straight stitching, covering the raw edges of the border fabric.

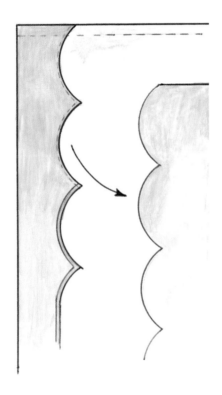

Hem the side edges of the border to be even with the side edges of the sheet.

Bordered Pillowcase
Follow the steps used for the sheet for the pillowcase, using design #44/40/39 as shown below.

Tasseled Throw

This cozy cover-up is a simple project that's easy to make using a lightweight upholstery fabric and wool/acrylic thread.

Finished size: 51" x 38" (129.5cm x 96.5cm)

Supplies

- 1¼ yards (1.15m) of 54" (137cm) wide home decorating fabric (make sure it fringes nicely)
- Monet embroidery thread in a coordinating color
- Topstitch needle #90/14 or 100/16
- Badgemaster water-soluble stabilizer
- Mega Hoop or largest hoop available for your machine
- Edgestitch foot (BERNINA® Foot #10/10C)
- Fabric marker

Using a fabric marker, draw lines 1½" (3.8cm) from selvage edges and 3" (7.7cm) from cut sides of fabric rectangle.

Adhere a layer of Badgemaster water-soluble stabilizer to the back of the fabric; hoop stabilized fabric in Mega Hoop. Set up machine with Monet thread in the needle and bobbin.

Embroider design #104 from Collection II along the cut edges of the fabric, aligning the center of the design on the marked 3" (7.7cm) line, and leaving 1½" (3.8cm) at each end for hemming the sides. Rehoop as necessary to embroider each long edge of the fabric rectangle.

When embroidery is complete, remove excess stabilizer and trim thread tails. Trim fringe, cutting loops.

Carefully fringe the fabric underneath the embroidered tassels.

Fold under ¾" (1.9cm) along each selvage edge; fold under an additional ¾" (1.9cm). Using an edgestitch foot (BERNINA® #10/10C), straight stitch along the inner fold to create double-fold hems at each side of the throw.

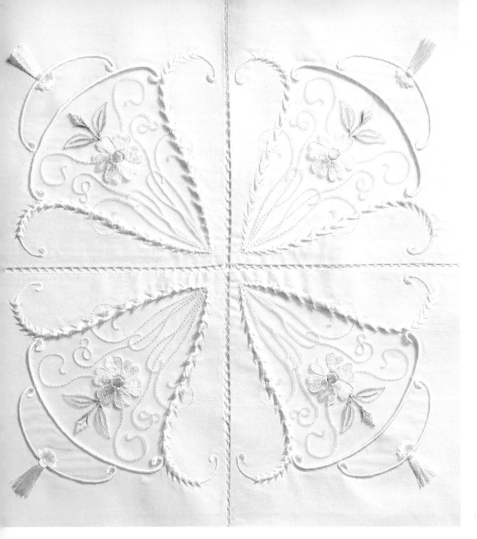

Overlay Appliqué Table Topper

This lovely topper lends grace and elegance to any table and features a unique bell-shaped design stitched as a sheer appliqué. The fagoted seams and the scalloped edging add to the old world charm of this beautiful table covering. See photos on pages 24 and 118.

Supplies

- 45" x 45" (1.14cm x 1.14cm) 100% white cotton fabric (pre-shrunk)
- 15" (40cm) white organza
- Stabilizers:
  Lightweight Tear-Away 2¼ yards (2m) water-soluble such as Aqua Film
- Threads:
  Isacord embroidery threads: as on the color chart included with the embroidery collection
  White embroidery thread for scallop hem
  Mettler 30 weight cotton embroidery thread
- Needles:
  Embroidery 75/11
  Sewing 80/12

- Feet:
  Fagoting or fringing foot (BERNINA® #7)
  Edgestitch foot (BERNINA® #10/10C)
  Embroidery foot (BERNINA® #15)
  Satin Stitch foot (BERNINA® #6)
- Embroidery Hoops: Large Oval and Medium
- CD rom Version BERNINA® *Tassels & Trims* Collection II or
  - #773 card version for smaller embroidery machines
- Fabric marker
- Small, sharp scissors
- Spray starch
- Seam sealant, such as *Fray Stoppa* by Helmar
- Long ruler

Preparation

Square the white cotton fabric. Fold in half and finger press lightly to establish the center. Fold in half again and repeat, again pressing lightly to mark with a crease.

Using a long ruler and a fabric marker, mark the creased lines and the center of the fabric.

Measuring from the intersection of the lines (center), mark a full 39½" (1m) circle. At this stage this will only be a guide. *Do not cut the circle on this line yet!*

Fagoting

On the straight lines only, cut the marked fabric into *four quarters.*

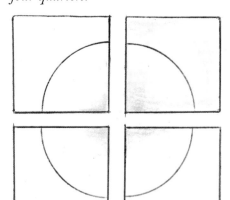

To stabilize the seams:

Spray starch all the new seam allowances (cut edges).

Press a small allowance (1/4"–6mm) to the back on each of these newly cut seams, taking care not to fray the edges.

Using an edgestitch foot (BERNINA® #10/10C), staystitch along the folded edges to stabilize them and help anchor the fagoting stitches on both sides.

To join the sections into a circle again, prepare as follows:

Cut two water-soluble stabilizer strips 3" (7.5cm) wide and the same length as the pressed edges.

Cut one water-soluble stabilizer strip 3" (7.5cm) wide and the full length across the half circle.

Place two of the fabric sections on top of one of the shorter strips of stabilizer, using pins or temporary spray adhesive to hold the fabric in place with the folded edges about 1/8" (3–4mm) apart. *Note: The distance between the sections to be joined depends on the width of the fagoting stitch. For this reason stitch a sample first and adjust the stitch width as needed; join all sections according to the sample width.*

Stitch the fagoting (see box) to join two quarter-circles to form a half-circle. Repeat with remaining two quarter-circles to form a second half-circle.

Using the longer strip of stabilizer, join the two half circles in the same manner to form a full circle.

After the stitching is complete, trim the threads and remove excess stabilizer. *Note: Stabilizer may be left in until all other stitching such as embroidery and scalloped edging have been completed. Then all stabilizer can be removed at the same time.*

Rinse in water to dissolve stabilizer. Let dry and carefully press the fagoted seams open. Lightly stretch the fagot seams open while pressing—*do not over stretch.*

Embroidery
Prepare the overlay for embroidery:

Using a fabric marker, draw a line 5" (12.8cm) from the outer edge of the topper as shown. This will be the placement line for stitching the scalloped edge.

Use templates to position and mark all embroidery placements as indicated in the embroidery directions on the following page.

←—5"—→

Fagoting
Fagoting or fringe foot (BERNINA® #7)
Feather or herringbone stitch
Mettler 30 weight cotton embroidery thread in the needle and bobbin

Place two folded or hemmed fabric edges on water-soluble stabilizer, leaving about 1/8" (3mm) of space between them.

Position the foot on the center of the stabilizer between the fabric edges. Adjust the length of the stitch to 1.5mm–2mm and the width so that the needle catches both folded fabric edge as it forms the stitch. Loosen the upper tension 2–3 notches if needed.

Tip: Stitch at a medium speed and keep the guide centered between the two pressed edges.

For *artista* embroidery machines:

Position large appliqué motif #90/76/– from Collection II, 2" (5cm) from the center of the overlay.

Hoop overlay with water-soluble stabilizer behind the fabric and white organza on the top.

Embroider appliqué motifs following the appliqué method in the instructions included with the collection. Repeat for each section of the overlay.

Position motif #89/75/– on the marked scallop edge; position the upper edge of the lower scroll on the marked line. Bond stabilizer to the wrong side using temporary spray adhesive and hoop the stabilized fabric. Stitch the design. Repeat for each section of the overlay.

Position motif #84/70/65 over the fagoted seams, 2" (5cm) from the marked hemline.

Add extra stabilizer to the back of fagoted seams for hooping. *Note: When hooping do not overstretch the fagoting.*

For other embroidery machines:
Note: If BERNINA® embroidery software is available, edit motif #87/73/68 (large scroll flower). Delete the scrolls on either side of the flower. Embroider only the flower 2" (5cm) from the center of the overlay. If no software is available, skip to next embroidery step.

Position motif #85/71/66–large tassel scallop–on the marked scallop edge.

Center motif #87/73/68–medium flower–over the fagoted seams, 2" (5cm) in from marked hemline.

Stitch all motifs as described. Remove excess threads and stabilizer. Cut tassels on the back and lift to the front.

Scalloped Edge
Finish the overlay with an elegant scalloped edge.

Set the machine for sewing the decorative scalloped hem:

White embroidery thread in the needle and white thread in the bobbin

Appliqué or Satin Stitch foot (BERNINA® #20/20C or #6)

To stabilize the hem:

Baste strips of stabilizer around the entire marked hem and/or spray starch the remaining edge *(do not spray on the pen markings; instead, stitch a basting line and remove later).*

On the *artista* 200E select scallop #416; other machines, select a satin stitch scallop. Test and adjust for a smooth satin stitch.

Stitch scallops on the marked hemline. Start at the edge of one of the large embroidered tassel scallops, stitching around and over the fagoted seam to the next tassel embroidery. Repeat for the remaining sections.

Neaten the stitched scallops, removing unwanted threads and excess stabilizer.

Apply two coats of seam sealant to the outer edge of the entire scalloped hem. *Move tassels out of the way.* Once dry, use small scissors to cut around the entire scallop hem, removing excess fabric.

Finishing
Carefully rinse the overlay to remove any pen markings and water soluble-stabilizer. Dry flat and press on the wrong side, opening fagot seams. Do not stretch the organza appliqué. Spray starch the entire overlay for a crisp, fresh look.

Tasseled Twin Set

This understated pullover top and matching cardigan have eye-catching trim along the lower edges featuring satin stitching, tassels, and beading.

Supplies

- 1¾ yards (1.60m) of 60" (150cm) wide heavy woven fabric
- *Tassels & Trims II* embroidery collection
- Isacord embroidery thread in desired colors
- Construction thread in a color and fiber compatible with fabric
- Lightweight Tear-Away or Aqua Mesh stabilizer
- Temporary spray adhesive such as 505
- Universal needles–size #80/12
- Embroidery needles–size #75/11
- Seam sealant such as *Fray Stoppa* by Helmar
- Edgestitch foot (BERNINA® Foot #10/10C)
- Bias Binder attachment (BERNINA® #84 with Binder Foot #94)–optional
- Small beads
- Serger with 4 cones of thread–optional

Preparation

Using the enclosed pattern in the appropriate size, trace the top pieces and jacket front pieces and sleeves onto the fabric; mark darts.

Roughly cut out each traced piece, allowing an extra 5" (12.8cm) along the lower edges, and an extra 2" (5.8cm) along the remaining edges.

Cut three yards of 2¼" (5.8cm) wide bias strips for binding.

Embroidery

Using temporary spray adhesive, bond stabilizer to the wrong side of the fabric pieces under the lower edge areas. Hoop the stabilized fabric.

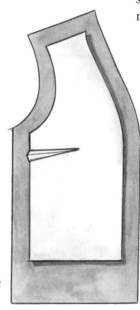

Select design #61/54/50 and stitch it as described below along the lower edges of the jacket front and sleeves edges and the lower edge of the top. Rehoop as needed to stitch completely across the edges.

Top: Stitch the satin zigzag border only, color 1, omitting the tassels. Once the hem has been completed, topstitch a triple straight stitch (length=3mm) in the same color ⅛"(3mm) above the embroidered border following the zigzag pattern. Repeat for the back.

Jacket: Front hem only–embroider the full motif with all the color changes.

Sleeves: Stitch color 1, with all the tassels. Remove the jump stitches between the tassels. Stitch color 2. Remove the connecting stitches between the tassels after the border has been completed. Stitch color 3, alternating the color of the tassels. Remove the connecting stitches between the tassels after the border has been completed.

Remove the stabilizer from the wrong side of the fabric pieces. Clip the bobbin threads and release the tassels on the jacket hem and sleeve edges.

Apply seam sealant to the jagged edges of the designs on all embroidered fabric pieces; let dry. Using sharp scissors, trim the excess fabric along the lower jagged edges of the embroidery, carefully avoiding the tassels.

Place pattern pieces on fabric, aligning stitched hems with hemlines of pattern pieces. Adjust placement of pattern pieces so that right and left sides of the hems are mirror images, with a "point" or "valley" in the center of each piece. Cut garment pieces from fabric.

Garment Construction–Top
Stitch darts in top front. Place the front and back right sides together and stitch or serge the shoulder seams.

Stitch or serge the side seams.

Fold bias strips in half lengthwise and press. Stitch binding to the right side of the neck edge, keeping raw edges even. Wrap the binding to the wrong side and stitch in place using an edgestitch foot (BERNINA® #10/10C).

Bind the armhole openings in the same manner.

Hand-sew wooden beads to the hem in the spaces at the top of the zigzag.

Garment Construction–Cardigan
Stitch darts in jacket front. Place the front and back right sides together and stitch or serge the shoulder seams.

Hem the back lower edge by turning it up ¹/₂" twice and stitching in place using an edgestitch foot.

Stitch or serge the side seams.

Stitch the sleeve seams; stitch the sleeves to the garment, easing in the fullness between the notches to create a smooth cap.

Fold bias strips in half lengthwise and press. Starting at one lower edge, stitch binding to the jacket opening, keeping raw edges even. Wrap the binding to the wrong side and stitch in place using an edgestitch foot.

Hand-sew wooden beads to the hem in the spaces at the top of the zigzag.

Embroidered Holiday Candle

An easy way to create a festive centerpiece (shown on page 56) using a plain white candle and a special holiday design.

Supplies

- Large white candle–about 4" (10cm) or larger in diameter
- Candle Podge or Mod Podge
- Straight pins
- Vinegar
- Small paintbrush
- Spray varnish
- Scraps of organza–large enough to fit in hoop–same color as candle
- Water-soluble stabilizer, such as OESD Aqua Film or Aqua Mesh
- Embroidery thread, including gold metallic thread for tassels
- Seam sealant, such as *Fray Stoppa* by Helmar
- Hand sewing needle

Directions

Red Border

Load border motif #20/17/12 or #29/–/– from *Tassels & Trims* Collection I.

Duplicate motif for a total of six units (very large candles may require additional units).

Rotate, move, and link the motifs to create a continuous trim as long as the hoop. *Note: Enough continuous trim is needed to go around the upper edge of the candle. Multiple hoopings will be required if using a smaller hoop or very large candle.*

Hoop a single layer of organza with water-soluble stabilizer in the Mega Hoop.

Insert a #75/11 Embroidery needle into the machine; red embroidery thread in needle, fine white thread in bobbin.

Embroider the complete border; remove the fabric from the hoop.

Treat the top and bottom edges of the stitched border with seam sealant. Let dry.

Trim organza from edges of embroidered trim. Press.

Center Tassel Motif

Load motif #12/12/12 from *Tassels & Trims II*.

Hoop one layer of white organza with water-soluble stabilizer in the medium hoop

Embroider motif #12/12/12, stitching colors 4 (tassels) and 6 (tinsel garland) with gold metallic thread.

Remove fabric from hoop; rinse until the embroidery is soft and all stabilizer is removed. Let dry.

On wrong side, clip tassels just below the bobbin threads. Pull tassels to front; neatly trim tassel ends.

Treat the entire outer edge of the embroidered motif with seam sealant. Let dry; press on wrong side.

Cut all fabric from around the treated edges. Carefully trim organza close to embroidery, taking care not to clip threads. Trim as much fabric as possible from inside the embroidery as well.

Assembly

Wipe candle with vinegar to remove excess grease.

Center the motif on the candle. To temporarily hold it in place, stick pins through the motif straight into the candle.

Pin the red continuous trim to the candle, 1/2" (1.5 cm) from the top edge, starting at the back and working around the front to the back again. Trim and fold under both ends; handstitch ends together.

Apply candle podge generously over the embroidered motifs, but *do not coat the tassels*–let them hang free from the embroidery.

Remove any air bubbles by rubbing gently with fingers. Let dry. Remove pins.

Apply two more coats of candle podge, allowing candle to dry between layers. When completely dry, spray with varnish.

Note: Do not burn candle. If desired, burn candle before starting the project to create a space large enough to hold a votive or tea candle.

chapter 9

The exploration continues, with fifty-seven exciting new tassel, fringe, floral and appliqué trims. Designed especially for this book, these embellishment motifs included in the Tassels & Trim Special Collection CD. To view the entire Special Collection of designs, see Appendix C on page 111.

Projects: Special Collection

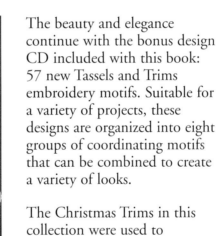

The beauty and elegance continue with the bonus design CD included with this book: 57 new Tassels and Trims embroidery motifs. Suitable for a variety of projects, these designs are organized into eight groups of coordinating motifs that can be combined to create a variety of looks.

The Christmas Trims in this collection were used to embellish the festive table linens detailed on the following pages and are also perfect adornments for tree skirts, wall hangings, and other holiday items. Another coordinated table dressing, shown on page 66, uses the Pretty Posies designs to trim a fringed table cloth and glass-topped tray, perfect for your next tea party!

The designs in the Special Collection are also wonderful for adding an elegant touch to garments. Pale blue Floral Ribbons—designs #6 and #7 —provide the perfect embellishment for a plain white pullover top made of crinkled cotton gauze, shown on page 69. Elegant tone-on-tone Tufted Swag embroidery, motifs #9-13, adds a rich, heirloom look to the Sheer Christening Dress on page 60.

The Renaissance belt motifs are unique stitched components that create a project as you stitch! Designed with stitched cutwork and reinforced with metal grommets at each end, these two motifs are trimmed after stitching is complete and then laced together to form an unusual belt. Stitch as many as you need for just the right size.

Sixteen blackwork squares make a designer chessboard, page 72, but can also be used to create an all-over patchwork pattern or interesting border for a variety of projects. The border motifs, plain or with long free-hanging tassels, offer a simple, yet striking finish to projects with straight sides such

Formal Tassel

This large, monochromatic tassel grouping has two motifs. The first, #14, is a tassel and ornament duo designed for easy and accurate linking. Use it to create long rows of tassels for borders and edge finishes. Motif #15 is a single tassel that can be used alone, scattered to create an all-over pattern, or combined with any border. This is one tassel you'll use again and again.

Holiday Table

This festive table starts with a square cloth covered with an oversized square topper, embellished with corner designs and sheer appliqués in red, green, and gold. *Note: Directions for the holiday candle shown in the photo on the previous page are in Chapter 8.*

as purses, scarves, table runners, etc. The open spaces within the diamond shapes can be filled with multi-color rhinestones or jewels for a rich, ornate look.

In addition to the designs used in the projects in this chapter, several additional motifs are included on the Special Collection CD, ready to be used in any way you can imagine!

Chinese Trim

The perfect trim to be stitched in a short time, motif #5 is designed for projects that have long, straight edges, such as bed linens and tablecloth borders. Link duplicates of this two-tone motif and in a short time a long line of wonderful tassels will complete your project.

Supplies

- 1³/₄ yard (1.6m) of 60" (150cm) red fabric
- 1¹/₂ yard (1.4cm) 54" (137cm) or 60" (150cm) green fabric
- Isacord embroidery threads
- Tear-Away stabilizer
- Temporary spray adhesive such as 505
- ¹/₄ yard (23cm) sheer fabric for appliqués
- Two spools of red sewing thread
- Two spools of green sewing thread
- Serger
- Three cones of red serger thread
- Three cones of green serger thread
- Double needle
- All-purpose foot (BERNINA® Foot #1/1C)

Red Tablecloth

55" x 55" (140cm x 140cm) finished size

Cut a 57" (144.8cm x 144.8cm) square of fabric. Serge-finish all four sides using a 3-thread balanced stitch.

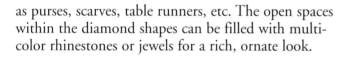

Turn under 1" (2.5cm) on all sides and press to crease; unfold. Hoop the tear-away stabilizer and attach the hoop to the machine. Spray the stabilizer with temporary adhesive. Smooth a corner of the unhemmed cloth onto the stabilizer, positioning the head of the tassel at the intersection of the creased lines.

When the stitching is finished, remove the stabilizer/fabric from the hoop. Clip the bobbin thread to release the tassel skirt and remove all excess stabilizer from the fabric.

Repeat the stitching of design #30 on the remaining three corners.

Press under 1" (2.5cm) on all sides, mitering and stitching the corners as shown. Pin or spray-baste the hem in place.

Insert a double needle and thread the machine with two spools of red thread. Hem cloth with double needle straight stitching along the upper edge of the hem allowance.

Green Table Topper
46" x 46" (117cm x 117cm) finished size

Cut a 47½" (120.7cm x 120.7cm) square of fabric. Serge-finish all four sides using a 3-thread balanced stitch.

Press under ¾" (1.9cm) on all sides, mitering and stitching the corners as previously shown. Pin or spray-baste in place.

Insert a double needle and thread the machine with two spools of green thread. Hem cloth with double needle straight stitching along the upper edge of the hem allowance.

Mark the centerlines and diagonals by folding and pressing light creases in the cloth.

Measure 34½" (88cm) from the center along each line—this marks the center of the embroidered, upside-down hearts in design #27.

Hoop the tear-way stabilizer and attach the hoop to the machine. Spray the stabilizer with temporary adhesive. Smooth the hemmed cloth onto the stabilizer, positioning it as needed.

Embroider design #27 from the Special Collection at the corner, midway between the center and the corner, placing a layer of sheer fabric over the embroidery area before stitching the first color. Trim the excess from around the outer edges of the stitching before continuing with the remaining colors.

Embroider a mirror imaged (upside down) scallop link design #29 between each of the previously embroidered motifs as shown on page 58.

When the stitching is finished, remove the stabilizer/fabric from the hoop. Trim away the green fabric from behind design #27, taking care not to cut the sheer fabric.

Sheer Christening Dress

This beautiful Christening dress with delicate embroidery embellishments is sure to become an heirloom in your family. Made with an organza overskirt, bodice and sleeves, the dress has dainty scallops with tufts along the hem, and flowers scattered on the bodice. The white-on-white embroidery adds simple elegance to the dress. See photo on page 120.

Supplies

- 1³/₄ yards (1.60m) 60" wide (150cm) white organza
- 1½ yards (1.30m) 45" wide (115cm) satin lining
- 7 small white buttons
- 4 yards (4m) ½" wide (1.5cm) white satin ribbon
- 19½" (50cm) white satin bias binding
- Threads:
  Fine white sewing thread (60 weight)
  White embroidery thread (Isacord)
  White bobbin thread (Metrolene)
- Presser Feet:
  Buttonhole foot
  (BERNINA® Foot #3A)
  Button sew-on foot
  (BERNINA® Foot #18)
  Embroidery foot
  (BERNINA® Foot #15)
  Edgestitch foot
  (BERNINA®Foot #10/10C)
  All-purpose foot
  (BERNINA® Foot #1/1C)
  Overlock foot
  (BERNINA® Foot #2/2A)
- Needles:
  Embroidery needle 75/11
  Universal needle 60/80
- Stabilizers:
  Lightweight Tear-Away stabilizer
  Water-soluble stabilizer such as Aqua Film
- Hoops:
  Medium hoop
  Large oval hoop
  Mega Hoop–optional
- *Tassels & Trims* Special Collection CD

Layout & Cutting

Pin all pattern pieces to the fabric as indicated below:
Organza:

> Bodice front (pleated front)–cut 1 on the fold
>
> Bodice back–cut 2
>
> Sleeves–cut 2
>
> Cuffs–cut 2
>
> Skirt–cut 1 on the fold—no facings on center back seam
>
> Tabs–cut 2

Trace all the above onto fabric, extending 6" (16cm) at skirt hemline and 2" (5cm) around the entire bodice. Trace the two tabs on a piece of fabric large enough for one hooping.

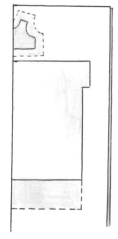

Trace the sleeve cuffs, cuff to cuff with 2" (5cm) extra around. Both sleeves can be hooped in the Large Oval hoop; center cuff fold lines to embroider the sleeves in one hooping. Cut out on new extended lines. DO NOT cut fabric pieces on the original pattern lines until ALL embroidery is complete.

Transfer all embroidery positions—X marks—from the pattern sheet.

Stitch a basting line on the skirt front and back to use as a guideline for the border embroidery.

Satin Lining

Skirt–cut 1 on the fold

Bodice front–cut 1 on the fold

Bodice back–cut 2

Embroidery

Set machine for embroidery

- Feed dog down
- White embroidery thread in needle
- Bobbin thread
- Embroidery foot
- Embroidery needle

Sleeves

Hoop the piece of organza with two sleeves traced on it with one layer of water-soluble stabilizer in the Large oval hoop. Center cuff seam lines with template centerlines.

Load motif #12–diamond with tuft. Move the motif to the (X) embroidery mark for the sleeve at the top of the hoop, parallel to the sleeve hem. Stitch motif.

Move the motif to the sleeve at the bottom of the hoop, then flip it horizontally so that the tassels face the hem. Stitch the motif. Remove from hoop. Remove any loose threads on the right and wrong side of the embroidered motifs. Set aside.

Front Bodice

Hoop the organza bodice front with water-soluble stabilizer in medium hoop; fabric should be completely flat. Load motif #11–small

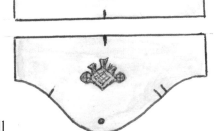

flower; embroider a few flowers at random on the center section between the marked tucks.

Tabs

On a scrap piece of organza, pin and trace the tab pattern piece two times. Mark embroidery locations with an X. Do not cut tabs apart. Hoop the complete piece of marked fabric in the medium hoop.

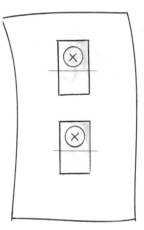

Load motif #13–circle link. Embroider two motifs on marked (X) spots. Remove from hoop. Remove any unwanted threads.

Organza Skirt

Load motif #9–medium scallops. Mirror horizontally to start the embroidery with the small flower. Plan the complete border using templates printed from the Special Collections CD. Mark the beginning/end of each section on the fabric. Hoop the organza skirt, using the stitched basting line as a guide and starting at the left back skirt. Embroider the first section of the border on the hem.

Rehoop, aligning the stitched basting line with the guideline again. Repeat the motif until the entire border has been embroidered, ending close to the back seam (border ends on a scallop).

Load motif #11—small flower, move motif until it lines up perfectly with the last scallop; overlap slightly and stitch. Remove from hoop. Remove all unwanted excess stabilizer and threads.

Unpick or clip all bobbin threads of the tiny tufts. Remove any loose threads. Remove the stabilizier, taking care not to damage the tiny tufts or the organza.

Rinse all embroidered pieces. Let dry; press lightly.

Cut all the embroidered pieces according to original pattern.

Construction
Set machine for sewing:
- Feed dog up
- White 60 weight thread in needle and bobbin
- Universal needle, size 60/8
- All-purpose foot

Bodice Front and Back
Fold tucks on both sides of organza front, pin in place; press and top stitch in place.

Baste organza bodice front to bodice front lining. Baste organza bodice back to lining backs. *Note: Handle each organza/lining bodice section as one piece of fabric.*

Stitch shoulder seams; press open. Overlock seam allowances using an overlock stitch and foot.

Sleeves
Stitch underarm seams. Overlock seam allowances and press seams open.

Easestitch both sleeves between the marked dots.

Cuffs
Fold the cuffs on foldlines, right sides together. Stitch the small darts. Clip close to the dots. The darts form a slit in the center of each cuff. Turn to right side and press only the slits.

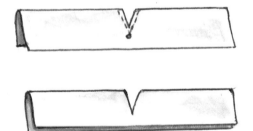

Fold right sides together again, to access the cuff underarm seams. Stitch seams. Fold to the right side; press the folds and the seams.

Pin the cuffs to the lower edges of sleeves. Matching the center notches, right side of cuff to *inside & wrong side* of sleeve, stitch in place. Overlock both cuff seams.

Fold the cuffs to the outside of the sleeves; press the cuffs upwards.

Setting the Sleeves
Pin the sleeves to the armholes, right sides together, easing in the fullness from dot to dot. Insert the sleeves; overlock the seam allowances of each sleeve together. Remove ease stitches.

Organza Skirt
On the organza skirt, pin both tucks horizontally on the marked lines. Topstitch along the marked stitching lines using a straight stitch with a length of 3.5mm; press both tucks toward the hem.

For the edge-to-edge seams on both center backs, fold under 1" (2.5cm). Overlock or fold under ¼" (6mm) to finish the raw edges. Press seams flat. Topstitch along the inner edge from the top to the hem.

Overlock the edge of the hem allowance. Fold the hem up until the overlock stitching meets the center of the embroidered scallops. Press the hem (fold) only. The hem can be sewn by machine or hand-stitched on the wrong side with a fine thread and needle.

Satin Skirt
On the skirt satin lining, stitch the center back seam from the dot down to the hem. Overlock the seam allowances together from the dot down to the hem; press.

Overlock the hem on the lower edge, fold under ¼" (6mm) along the raw edge; topstitch in place.

Back Opening
Press the back seams as follows:

Left Bodice Back (left side facing up). Starting at the neck edge, fold the facing on the fold line. This side will be wider than the right side and forms the wider facing for the buttonholes.

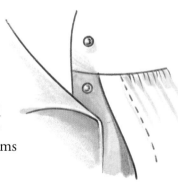

Right Bodice Back (right side facing up). Fold under 1" (2.5cm) on the facing line. This fold will not meet the center back seam; it forms an extended buttonstand. When the left back is buttoned over the right back, the organza layers of the skirt will meet edge to edge at the center back.

The left satin bodice back will close 1" (2.5cm) over the extended button stand.

Adjust the facing folds if they do not align perfectly. Press both seams.

Joining the Skirts

Fold the pressed satin seams open again before pinning and stitching the skirt sections together.

Pin the finished organza skirt to the satin skirt as follows:
Start at the center fronts, working toward the back seam opening. Left back–on the buttonhole side of the satin lining, pin the organza up to the pressed edge, then fold the satin facing open again.

Right back–on the lining, pin the organza skirt edge 1" (2.5cm) from the facing fold. Open the extended button stand again.

Stitch two rows of gathering stitches between the notches at the top edge of each skirt panel, through all layers. Gather the skirt to fit the bodice front and back, matching center fronts, side seams, notches and center back opening.

Sew the waistline seam. Overlock the seam allowances together. Press seam toward the bodice. Overlock both center back seams from neckline to skirt seams.

Fold back previously pressed back opening edges. The left side will close over the right back bodice and skirt while the organza skirt will meet edge to edge. The organza skirt will be open from the bodice seam to the hem. *Note: With an open organza center back seam the dress looks fuller without having lots of extra fabric.*

Skirt lining only–reinforce the end of the opening at the center back seam by stitching across both lining seams. This will keep the overlap in place as well.

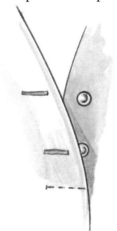

Finishing the Dress

Pin the satin bias binding to the neck edge. Open the binding, then pin the *right side* of the smaller seam allowance to the *wrong side* of the neck edge. Stitch around the neckline. Tuck in the edges; fold the binding to the right side, just covering the first stitching line. Edgestitch using an edgestitch foot.

Sew five buttonholes on the left side of the back opening, 1 1/4" (3cm) apart.

Sew two buttonholes on the lower skirt lining— *not on the organza.* Match button positions with buttonholes on the right side of the back bodice; sew on the buttons using a button sew-on foot (BERNINA® #18).

Fold the embroidered organza in half, right sides together. Stitch seam on one side on the edge; turn right side out and press, centering embroidery. Fold in 1/4" (6mm) at the top and bottom edges; pin the tabs to the center of the front bodice tucks with the lower edges 1/4" (6mm) below the waistline seam. Topstitch both tabs in place.

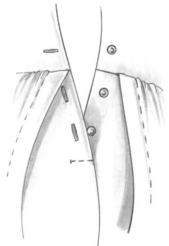

Sew four thread loops by hand around the bodice seam: one at each side seam, and one on each side of the center back.

Cut ribbon into two pieces. Loop one half through the two front tabs and side seam thread loops, matching the center of the ribbon with the center front of the bodice. Loop the other half through the back loops. Tie ends of ribbons into bows at the side seams. Shorten the ribbon ends, if needed, so that they hang even with the skirt tucks.

Renaissance Belt

Two easy, monochrome embroidery motifs—one for the center fronts and the other for linking—complete this unusual tied denim belt. The cutwork diamond shapes add a special touch to the finished belt. Adjust the lace-up sides as needed for a comfortable fit on your hips, or add additional linking sections for a longer length. No sewing skills are needed to complete this trendy belt.

Denim Belt

Supplies

- Fabrics:
  12" x 60" (30cm x 150cm) heavy, dark blue denim

  12" x 60" (30cm x 150cm) dark blue cotton for lining
- Approximately 4–5 yards (3.70m) leather strips for lacing–approximately 3/16" (5mm) wide
- Embroidery thread (one color)
- Bobbin thread
- Size #90/14 Embroidery needles
- Seam sealant, such as *Fray Stoppa* by Helmar
- 1 packet of brass eyelets–medium size (26 eyelets for size 8 belt)
- Wooden beads in assorted sizes–optional

- Temporary adhesive such as 505 spray
- Small sharp scissors
- BERNINA® *artista* 200E
- Large Oval hoop
- Eyelet punch such as found in the BERNINA® Eyelet Embroidery Set #82
- Embroidery Wand–optional

Preparation

Decide on the number of links needed to complete your belt. The denim belt shown—two fronts plus four links—fits an approximate size 8 waist (specific measurements on the following page).

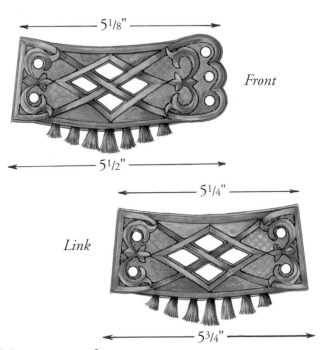

Front

Link

Measurement of
Upper Edge of Front = 5 1/8" (13.1cm)
Upper Edge of Link = 5 1/4" (13.4cm)

Lower Edge of Front = 5 1/2" (14cm)
Lower Edge of Link = 5 3/4" (14.6cm)

Belt measurements below are based on the upper edge of the belt:

4 Link Belt = (2 fronts) + (4 links)–fits up to 37" (94cm)

5 Link Belt = (2 fronts) + (5 links)–fits up to 42" (107cm)

6 Link Belt = (2 fronts) + (6 links)–fits up to 47" (119.5cm)

Embroidery

Lightly spray wrong side of denim with temporary adhesive. Adhere to cotton lining, wrong sides together. Hoop the denim/lining snugly in the Large Oval Hoop (or largest hoop available).

Select center front motif (#24) from the Special Collection CD. Embroider one time. Engage Vertical Mirror Image; embroider one time. Select link motif (#25); embroider required number of links, rehooping fabric as needed. *Note: Multiple motifs can be positioned and stitched using* **artista** *On-Screen Editing functions.*

Once all sections have been embroidered, remove hoop from machine and fabric from hoop. Remove excess stabilizer and clip thread tails. Cut between sections to create smaller sections for easier handling.

Clip the tassels on the wrong side just below the bobbin threads. Using the Embroidery Wand, carefully release the lower edge of the tassels on the front of each section.

Apply seam sealant to the four inner sides of the satin stitched diamonds, and around the outer edges of each section, including underneath the tassels. Let dry, then press embroidery from the wrong side. Neaten the tassels with a little steam, and then trim the lower edges.

Using small, sharp scissors cut all the embroidered motifs close to the treated edges. Cut away the fabric from inside the four inner diamonds of each section, taking care not to damage any of the satin stitches.

Construction

Using an eyelet embroidery set, punch holes for eyelets as follows:

- Center front edges–one eyelet centered in each of the three scallops
- All other edges–one eyelet centered in each scroll (two on each end of each section)

Following manufacturer's instructions, insert brass eyelets into each punched hole.

Add 1 to the number of links in the belt. Cut this many strips of leather, each 17" (43cm) long. Use one strip to lace two links together. Trim to desired length.

Optional: Thread beads onto laces before trimming ends. Use remaining leather strip to lace center fronts together.

Lace fronts and trim ends of leather lacing to desired length.

Variation: Imitation Leather Belt

Substitute imitation leather for denim; belt may be self-lined or lined with cotton as for denim belt.

Make this belt using the directions for the Denim Belt with the following changes:

Use a Jeans needle #90/14 when sewing and embroidering imitation leather.

Omit the grid embroidery (first step) for the link sections.

Cut two thin strips (60" x ½" or 150cm x 1.2cm), across the width of the fabric. Fold in half lengthwise and edgestitch using an edgestitch foot (BERNINA® #10/10C). Set aside; use for lacing the front edges together.

Trim sections as for denim belt, but do not trim short ends. Extend these 1½" (4cm) beyond satin stitching and shape as shown in the diagram below.

Join links using silver rings or buckles:

- Thread shaped extension through ring
- Fold to the back, then fold under a small hem, ⅛" to ¼" (3mm to 6mm)
- Use a zipper foot (BERNINA® #4) to stitch hem in place (buckle should be free to move)

Complete center fronts as for Denim Belt, substituting six silver eyelets for brass eyelets.

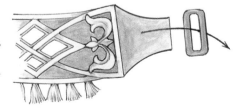

Pretty Posies Tea Table

Exotic fringed flowers and corner designs with tiny tufts embellish this linen tablecloth. Link related designs to stitch a tea tray insert to have a truly coordinated table for that special occasion. See photo on page 118.

Tablecloth
Supplies
- Fabric:
  60" x 60" (150cm x 150cm) white table linen
- Thread:
  Isacord embroidery thread
  White construction thread
  White bobbin thread
- Filler cord (or gimp cord) for pintucks
- Needles:
  Universal #80/12
  Embroidery #75/11
  Double needle 4.0/80
- Pintuck foot (BERNINA® Foot #31–5 grooves)
- Embroidery foot (BERNINA® Foot #15)
- All-purpose foot (BERNINA® Foot #1/1C)
- *Tassels & Trims* Special Collection CD
- Embroidery Wand–optional
- *artista* 200E
- Mega Hoop
- Large Oval hoop
- Medium hoop
- Stabilizer such as Lightweight Tear-Away by OESD
- Temporary adhesive such as 505
- Spray starch
- Water-soluble marker

Preparation
Wash and press the fabric before use.

Fold fabric in half vertically; press lightly to mark the vertical center of the fabric; unfold. Fold in half horizontally; mark the horizontal center of the fabric; unfold.

Using the enclosed pattern and a fabric marker, transfer the embroidery placement information and the double needle stitching lines. Mark the hem and fringing lines. *Do not cut fabric at this time!*

Embroidery—Center Block
Adhere a layer of stabilizer to the wrong side of the linen, behind the marked center, using temporary fabric adhesive. Hoop the fabric/stabilizer in the Mega Hoop, and then attach the hoop to the embroidery module.

Load design #19 from the Special Collection CD. Check design to see if it will be stitched in the correct spot; adjust position of motif as needed.

Stitch the first half of the center block; when stitching is complete, remove fabric from hoop. Turn tablecloth 180°, rehoop, and check to see that motifs are aligned correctly. Adjust as needed, then stitch the second half of the block motif.

Rehoop, using Medium hoop. Load motif #20 (linking circle) and center it between the opposite sides of the previously stitched Mega Hoop motifs. Repeat for the other side of the center block. When embroidery is complete, remove fabric from hoop, Gently tear away stabilizer and clip threads tails.

Alternate Instructions for Embroidering the Center Block using the Large Oval Hoop instead of the Mega Hoop

Follow the pattern diagram to create the center block:

- Hoop fabric and stabilizer in the Large Oval hoop.
- Select motif #16, the corner motif, and stitch four times to build the center block, rehooping as needed.
- Select motif #20, the circle link, and stitch four times centered between the corner motifs to complete the center block.

Embroidery—Corners

Hoop fabric and stabilizer in Large Oval hoop.

Load motif #16 and stitch in each of the four marked corner positions, rehooping as needed.

When stitching is complete, remove fabric from hoop, remove all stabilizer, clip thread tails and jump stitches.

Decorative Double Needle Work

Remove the embroidery module and set machine for sewing—feed dog up, Double needle, pintuck foot, two spools of thread (placed so they unwind in opposite directions), and white bobbin thread.

Tip: Before starting pintucks, prepare a few extra bobbins to ensure finishing the pintucks without interruptions.

Thread the Double needle and insert the gimp cord up through the stitch plate following the instructions in the machine manual.

Select straight stitch and adjust the stitch length to 2mm. Using a scrap piece of the same fabric as the tablecloth, stitch a pintuck sample and adjust the needle tension as necessary.

Stitch the pintucks, starting at the center block and following the transferred lines.

After stitching the center area, stitch a double row of pintucks along the outer edges following the marked lines.

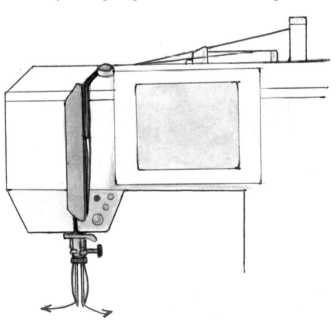

Stitching Corners

Stop the machine at each corner, needles down. Raise the presser foot, then turn fabric 45°. Lower the presser foot, take one stitch (turning the flywheel by hand) with the inner needle stitching through the same spot as in the previous stitch. With the needles down, raise the presser foot, turn the fabric again to complete the corner, lower the presser foot, and continue stitching.

Clip the Tassels

Tiny Tufts–Carefully remove only the bobbin threads (the tufts will be too short if they are cut).

Flowers–Carefully cut the fringe on the back close to the bobbin threads (or gently remove the bobbin threads). *Take care not to damage the embroidery stitches under the fringe.* Steam flowers on the right side and fluff with your fingers.

Fringing Finish

Following the marked hemline, below the corner embroideries, remove a thread on all four sides of the tablecloth. To do this, pick up a thread in the middle of one side using the Embroidery Wand, then pull it toward one side of the tablecloth. Remove only one thread on each of the four sides. These will be the guidelines for sewing the blanket stitch before fringing the edges.

Spray starch the hem area and press carefully before stitching.

Insert a Universal needle and attach an all-purpose foot (BERNINA® #1/1C) to the machine. Stitch along pulled thread lines using a blanket stitch and white thread, stopping at each corner. Lower needle at the corner, turn fabric 90°, and continue to the next corner. Repeat until all four sides are stitched.

Rinse tablecloth to remove all the transferred lines. Press on the wrong side.

Trim the hem to desired length before fringing. *Only at this stage start to fray the edges.* Beginning at the outer edge and working toward the blanket stitch, remove threads one at a time. Pick up each thread in the center (the Embroidery Wand is very helpful for this step) and pull it toward one side. Continue until all threads between the blanket stitch and raw edge have been removed. Press tablecloth again on the wrong side.

Tea Tray

Supplies

- Round, oval, or octagonal tray
- White table linen (same as tablecloth)–about 2"–3"(5cm–7cm) larger than tray on all edges
- Isacord embroidery thread
- Stabilizer such as Lightweight Tear-Away by OESD
- Temporary adhesive such as 505 spray
- Glass cut to fit inside the tray
- Clear silicone sealant

Preparation

To create a pattern, trace the shape of your tray using a fabric marker. Draw a line 1¹/₂" (3cm) from the outer edge to designate the start of the fringed border.

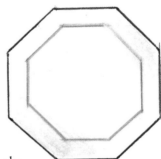

After printing templates from the CD, plan a round or oval border using the following motifs:

- #17–half circle
- #18–single flower
- #20–circle link

Embroidery

Adhere a layer of stabilizer to the wrong side of the linen using temporary fabric adhesive. Hoop the fabric/stabilizer, and then attach the hoop to the embroidery module.

Stitch the complete design on the insert, rehooping as needed.

When stitching is complete, remove fabric from hoop, remove all stabilizer, clip thread tails and jump stitches. Clip the flowers to create fringe following directions in Chapter 5.

Measure the fringe line around the outer edge of the octagonal tray liner. Cut a strip of fabric this length by 1¹/₂" (3cm), on the straight grain of the fabric. Sew a line of stay-stitching ¹/₄" (4mm) from one long edge; this is the stitching guide line. Cut strip into eight equal pieces and pin one to each side of the tray liner. Sew in place, using the stay-stitching as a guide. Trim both seam allowances (liner underneath and fringe strip above) close to stitching. Cover raw edge with a wide satin stitch. Fringe as directed for tablecloth.

Assembling the Tea Tray

Following the instructions on the package, apply clear silicone sealant inside the tray, along the entire bottom edge. Reapply, layer upon layer, to create a ¹/₄" (6mm) wide "shelf" for supporting the glass top. The "shelf" must be the same height as the fringed flowers so they won't be "squashed" when the glass is installed in the tray. When shelf is complete and sealant is dry, trim the entire edge with a sharp craft knife to create a smooth line. Remove any excess sealant.

Steam the tray cloth. Fluff the fringed flowers.

Spray a thin layer of spray adhesive on the bottom of the tray to keep the cloth in place. Carefully position the cloth liner in the tray, gently smoothing it in place. Trim the fringed edges if needed to make the inset the same size as the bottom of the tray.

Place the glass top (cut slightly smaller than the inside dimensions of the tray) on the silicone "shelf." Seal with silicone sealant, removing any excess.

Trimmed Gauze Top

Two pastel-colored tassel trims are stitched on a sheer, crinkled cotton gauze top. These tiny cascading tassels in pastel hues will enhance any project—from garments to the daintiest linen, or scattered close to the edges of a curtain border. Exchange the soft pastels for vibrant jewel tones for an entirely different effect. Add the coordinating single flower motif for even more design possibilities.

Materials

- 1³/₄ yards (1.60m) x 60" wide (150cm) white, crinkled cotton gauze
- White construction thread, such as Mettler Silk-Finish 100% cotton thread

Materials (continued)

- Embroidery thread in pastel colors (see color chart)
- Lightweight Tear-Away or Aqua Mesh stabilizer
- Size #70/10 Universal needles
- Size #75/11 Embroidery needles
- Water-soluble marking pen (test on scrap fabric before marking on project)
- Bias tape maker–medium size

Preparation

Pre-wash and press fabric before cutting.

Layout & Cutting

Allow an additional 6" (15cm) at each bodice lower front and upper sleeve lower edge for hooping. These extra allowances are included in the fabric requirements. Trace these pattern pieces onto the fabric, then mark extra allowances—trace these pattern pieces onto the fabric, then add extra allowances and cut on the new lines. These pieces will be trimmed to size after embroidery is complete.

    Cut 2 upper bodice fronts

    Cut 1 lower bodice, + extra allowance, placed on fold

    Cut 1 upper bodice back, placed on fold

    Cut 1 lower back + extra allowance, placed on fold

    Cut 2 upper sleeves + allowance

    Cut 4 lower sleeves

    Cut 1 bias strip 55" x 1" wide (1.40m x 2.5cm wide) for neck edge

    Cut 1 bias strip 45" x 1" wide (1.20m x 2.5cm wide) for sleeve ties

For a shorter top—shorten lower bodice back and lower bodice front 4" (10cm) at hemlines.

Embroidery

After stabilizing the fabric, hoop the top edge of the bodice lower front and attach the hoop to the machine. Select design #8 from the Special Collection CD; embroider at the upper edge of the bodice lower front.

Hoop the lower edge of the upper sleeve pieces using design #9 from the Special Collection CD.

Remove embroidered fabric from the machine and remove fabric from hoop. Carefully remove excess stabilizer and clip thread tails. Take care when removing stabilizer around the tiny tassels, as they can be damaged very easily. Dry press embroidery lightly from the wrong side.

Construction

All seam and hem allowances are included–1/2" (1.2cm).

Set machine for straight stitch:
- Feed dog raised
- #70/10 or #80/12 Universal needle
- White Silk-Finish cotton thread in needle and bobbin
- Sewing bobbin case

Staystitch bodice front and back necklines 1/4" (6mm) from raw edges.

With right sides together, stitch upper bodice center fronts together as below marking for center front opening. Press seam open and press under 1/2" (1.2cm) along center front opening. Overlock raw edges using a 2- or 3-thread serger overlock stitch, adjusting differential feed to avoid stretching the crinkled fabric.

Pressing Crinkled Fabrics

Dry press using medium heat after covering embroidery, seams and overlocking with a clean piece of white fabric. Lay fabric on top & press lightly, not too long. Do not stretch the fabric. Let fabric cool before moving.

Correct Hooping & Handling of Crushed/Crinkled Fabrics

- Unscrew hoop screws completely.
- Bond two layers of stabilizer to wrong side of fabric using temporary spray adhesive. Do not smooth fabric; keep natural creases in place.
- Hoop fabric/stabilizer.
- Replace inner hoop.
- Place plastic hoop template on fabric and carefully position fabric without stretching, taking care not to distort the natural crinkles.
- Tighten screws.

Do not trim any fabric from seam allowance while serging.

Topstitch 3/8" (1 cm) from both sides of center slit using a 3mm to 3.5mm long straight stitch.

With right sides together, stitch lower bodice front to upper bodice front. Press seam toward upper front; overlock raw edges. Topstitch. Repeat with lower bodice back and upper bodice back.

Join shoulder seams; press open and overlock.

Sew both side seams above side slit markings. Backstitch at the markings to reinforce the ends of the slit openings. Snip the front part of the enclosed seam to the stitching to allow both seam allowances to be pressed toward the back of the garment. Press and overlock seams together above the side slits; press the side slit hem allowances under. Topstitch around both side seam slits.

Sew the upper sleeves underarm seams, press and overlock seams together.

Sew the underarm seams for the two lower sleeves. Press and overlock seams together. Overlock both center slit seams; fold under 1/2" (1.2cm) hem and topstitch. Pin to upper sleeves, matching underarm seams and slits with center of sleeves. Stitch, overlock seams together and press toward upper sleeves. Topstitch.

Easestitch both sleeve heads by sewing a single line of 3mm long straight stitches between the notches. Pin finished sleeves to armholes, adjusting the ease as needed and inserting pins no more than 1/4" (6mm) apart. The closer together the pins are, the easier it will be to keep the eased sections in place when stitching. Using a 2.5mm long straight stitch, sew in the sleeves, stitching slowly when sewing the pinned sleeve heads, and removing each pin just before it goes under the presser foot. Overlock seams together; press towards the armholes.

Create bias binding using a bias tape maker, pressing the folded edges.

Tip: Before pressing the binding with the bias tape maker, spray fabric with spray starch. Shape folded binding while still warm.

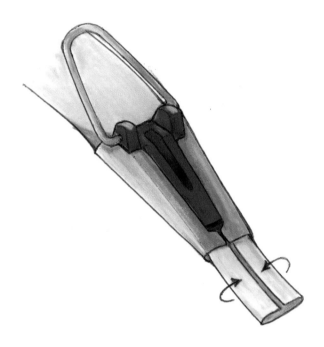

Center a 55" (1.40m) length of bias binding on center back neck, pinning right side of binding to wrong side of side of neck edge. Beginning at the center back, stitch binding around neckline, over the shoulder seams to the center front. Repeat for the other side. Fold raw edge of binding under, wrong sides together, then fold to right side of neck edge. Topstitch binding in place at neckline; continue stitching to ends of binding. Knot and trim both ends of center front ties.

Stitch ties for center of sleeves. Fold bias strip in half, topstitch along folded edge, press. Cut into two equal pieces. Tie a bow in each piece, knot ends, and trim. Stitch bows to centers of sleeves, just beneath embroidery and over the slits of the lower sleeves.

Fold under 1/2" (1.2cm) hem allowances at lower edge of bodice. Overlock raw edges; topstitch in place.

- Needles:
  Embroidery needle 90/14
  Universal needle 80/12
- Presser Feet:
  Embroidery foot (BERNINA® #15)
  All-purpose foot
  (BERNINA® #1/1C)
  Edgestitch foot
  (BERNINA® #10/10C)
- Stabilizer:
  Lightweight Tear-Away stabilizer
  Temporary spray adhesive such as 505
- Hoops:
  Large Oval hoop
  Mega Hoop (*artista* 200E)
  Large hoop–optional
- Water-soluble fabric marker
- Small sharp scissors
- Glass top ⅛" (3mm) thick cut to project finished size

Chessboard

Build a chessboard using unique blackwork embroidery designs from the BERNINA® Designer Plus version 4.0 embroidery software. This exceptional, easy project can be stitched on any embroidery machine, as individual pieces are stitched together using the sewing machine.

Chessboard finished size–13½" x 13½" (34.2cm x 34.2cm) *Note: The size of the finished chessboard may vary slightly from machine to machine because of the satin stitching.*

Supplies
- Fabrics:
  19½" x 45" (50cm x 115cm) medium-heavy loosely woven table linen
  16" x 16" (40cm x 40cm) white cotton
  16" x 16" (40cm x 40cm) white felt
- Threads:
  Black embroidery thread
  Black bobbin thread
  White embroidery thread
  White bobbin thread
  White sewing thread

Embroidery
Embroider the following on the white linen using the instructions below. The motifs will be embroidered, then cut apart and stitched together patchwork fashion.

Stabilize and hoop the fabric, starting at one end of the complete fabric strip. Rehoop until all of the embroidery motifs have been stitched. Replace or change stabilizer with each hooping as needed, making sure the fabric is hooped tautly.

Embroider 64 squares using black thread on the white woven linen with the following:
- Embroider each of the sixteen "black" squares—motifs #32–47 twice, arranging as many as possible in the hoop to minimize the number of hoopings. Leave ½" (1.2cm) between squares for "fine-tuning" later. Continue until all 32 "black" squares are complete.
- Load the plain square (motif #48). Embroider this motif 32 times. Total "black" and "white" squares embroidered = 64.
- Rehoop linen; stitch plain and fringed border components as listed below:

  Mega Hoop—see Diagram A—motif #52 two times; #57 two times
  Large Hoop/Large Oval Hoop—see Diagram B—motif #50 two times; #51 four times; #53 four times; #54 two times; #65 four times

- Do not stitch the same design next to the first one as the fabric might have shifted during stitching of this large design. For best results, rehoop, as the fabric needs to be taut for the next motif.
- Total borders needed = 4 (two plain and two tasseled)

Clip the tassels from the back. With the embroidery wand, release threads carefully from the front. Steam lightly. Trim all tassels to one length, making sure that no loop ends show.

Apply a few coats of seam sealant around the edges of all 64 squares. Let dry.

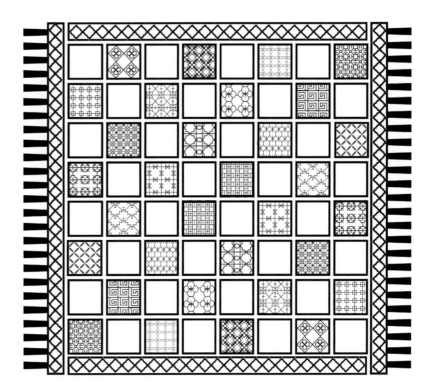

Diagram A: Mega Hoop

Trimming the Squares
Tips:
- Cut the embroidered squares apart, leaving a narrow edge (approximately 1/4" [6mm]) around all sides for easier handling; pieces will be trimmed to size later.
- Remove stabilizer from the blackwork squares only. The stabilizer left behind the plain squares will provide "padding" for these pieces.
- Press all embroidery from the wrong side.

Squares
Cut out all 64 squares (32 blackwork and 32 plain) with a 1/16" (2.5mm) edge on all four sides. Take care not to fray the narrow, treated edges.

Borders
Trim the border pieces for the narrow seams as follows:
- Leave 1/8" (3mm) along one long black satin stitch edge. Apply seam sealant to this edge.
- Leave 1/8" (3mm) seam on short sides (ends). Apply seam sealant to these edges.
- Leave a 1/2" (1.2cm) hem seam allowance along the outer tassel side.
- Leave a 1/2" (1.2cm) hem seam allowance along the outer plain side.

Arranging the Squares
Using a fabric marker, divide the white cotton fabric into four quadrants, drawing horizontal and vertical centerlines. These lines will help when arranging the squares in straight lines.

Spray temporary adhesive on one side of the white cotton. This will be the backing for the embroidered chessboard.

Following the apporopriate diagram, and starting in the center of the fabric, arrange the squares on the cotton backing, one blackwork and one plain square at a time. Overlap the edges so that each plain edge touches the black satin stitch edge of the next square; press in place. Continue in this manner until all the blocks are set (8 rows x 8 rows). *Tip: Spray more adhesive as you continue building the chessboard.* Take care not to fray any of the narrow edges. *Do not cut the cotton backing smaller at this stage!*

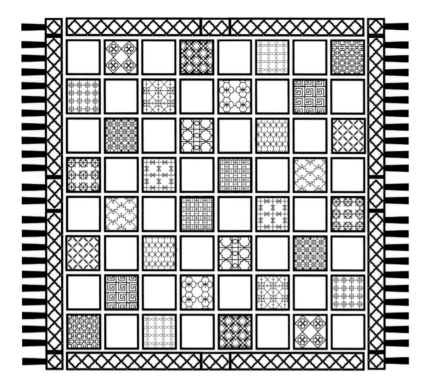

Diagram B: Large or Large Oval Hoop

Joining the Squares

Set the machine for sewing:

- Feed dog up
- Universal needle
- White embroidery thread
- White bobbin thread
- Edgestitch foot (BERNINA® #10/10C)
- Zigzag stitch–width and length 1.5mm
- Reset tension if previously adjusted for embroidery

Starting in the center of the chessboard, zigzag all the squares together. Take care not to fray the edges while joining the squares. Stitch from the top to the other end opposite side. Continue until all rows have been stitched together both horizontally and vertically.

After all the squares have been stitched together, sew two more times over the first stitching (total of three stitchings). Start with an open zigzag with a width of 1.5mm, changing to a slightly wider and finer satin stitch for the second stitching, and ending with a satin stitch with a width of 2.5mm, the same width as the black satin stitch border of

the embroidered squares. This stitching will cover the overlapping seam allowances. *Tip: If needed, adjust the last stitching to be slightly wider than 2.5mm.*

Borders

Check the border length of all four sides of the finished blackwork section. The four outer edges will be satin stitched after the embroidered borders have been attached.

Using the same method used to join the individual squares, stitch the border components together to create two plain and two fringed borders. *Note: Mega Hoop borders are already complete.*

Join the two tassel borders: with the tassels away from the board, pin the fringed borders to the last two raw edges of the connected squares. Attach using the same satin stitch technique used above.

Trim the raw edges of the cotton base fabric; fold to the back leaving a white edge, *not more than 1/8" (3mm)*, as a border around the entire chessboard, including under the tassel edges. Press carefully.

Trim the felt square to the exact size as the embroidered chessboard. Spray one side of the felt with temporary adhesive. Place the embroidered section on top and press in place. With a straight stitch (2mm length), sew next to the black embroidered satin stitches around all four sides, through all layers. Change to black thread on top only when sewing the tassels sides. Stitch over the tassels close to the black satin stitches. *Tip: While stitching the tassel borders, use the Embroidery Wand or a knitting needle to hold the tassels out of the way and prevent stitching over the free-hanging fringe.*

Use the same technique to straight stitch between the squares and along the inner edges of the four borders.

If necessary, trim the felt to the size of the top embroidery section.

For the final touch, and to protect the chessboard, cover with a glass top cut to size.

Shaped Valance and Bordered Curtain

Create a custom look for your windows with this surprising combination of sheer voile and sturdy denim. The shaped valance is trimmed with mini-piping and embroidered tassels that coordinate with the beautiful border stitched along the hem of the curtain.

Supplies

Note: The curtain and valance for this project can be made for any window (see page 76). Measurements shown are for a 36" (92 cm) wide window.

- Voile: see cutting instructions to determine yardage
- Denim (valance): 45" (115cm) wide x 22" (60cm)
- Cotton lining for valance: 45" (115cm) wide x 19" (50cm)
- Decorative curtain rod to fit window [diameter = 1" (2.5cm)]
- Contrasting piping–1 packet: 3³/₄ yards (3.5 meters)
- Lightweight Tear-Away stabilizer
- Adhesive-backed paper such as OESD Stabil-Stick
- Water-soluble stabilizer, such as OESD Aqua Film or Aqua Mesh
- Isacord embroidery thread
- Fine bobbin thread for embroidery, color to match voile
- Construction thread such as Mettler Metrosene Plus polyester thread
- Embroidery needles–#75/11 for voile, #90/14 for denim
- Universal needles–#60/8 for voile, #80/12 for denim
- Large Oval hoop
- Medium hoop
- Mega Hoop–optional
- Zipper foot (BERNINA® Foot #4) *or* piping foot (BERNINA® Foot #12)
- Embroidery foot (BERNINA® #15)

- All-purpose foot (BERNINA® #1/1C)
- Edgestitch foot (BERNINA® #10/10C)
- Small, sharp scissors
- Appliqué or duckbill scissors
- Water-soluble pen (pre-test on fabric)
- Flower-shaped beads in 2 colors–optional
- Embroidery Wand–optional

Curtain Preparation

Pre-wash and press fabrics to remove any creases.

Cut sides, bottom and top edges straight along grain lines. To do this, pull a warp and a weft thread (the full length) close to the frayed edges. Use this as a guide to cut all edges straight.

Curtain Layout & Cutting

Determine the total *length* required for each panel:

- Total Length = desired finished length + 2" (5cm) top seam + 8" (20cm) hem

Determine the total *width* required for the window:

- Total Width = 2½ times the width of the window (in this case, 90" (2.25 meters). If necessary, seam two or more fabric widths together to create wider panels. Divide the total width by the width of the voile; round up to the nearest whole number. This is the number of fabric lengths required for your window. Seam the widths together to make one piece of fabric 2½ times the width of the window

Mark the hemline horizontally across the lower edge of the panel, 8" (20cm) from bottom edge. Fold the hem up along the marked line; baste it in place using a straight stitch with a length of 3.5mm.

Mark the position of the continuous border 6½" (17cm) above the folded hem. This will be the center line for the border embroidery. Stitch a line of basting along this line.

Referring to the photo on page 74, load design #2 and/or #3 from the Special Collection CD, aligning each motif with the basted center line. Embroider the first color. *Note: The running stitches that form the base of the motifs should embroider without puckering—loosen needle tension slightly if needed.*

Clip thread tails, jump stitches, bobbin thread, and any other unwanted threads before stitching the next color, otherwise they will be difficult to remove and will show through the finished panel.

Continue embroidering, clipping threads between each color. Repeat, linking motifs (overlapping slightly). Continue stitching motifs, rehooping as needed until the entire lower edge of the panel has been embroidered. *Note: If desired, begin and end the continuous border with the single flower (design #1).*

Once the entire border has been embroidered, remove the basting stitches and clip any remaining unwanted threads. Carefully cut most of the stabilizer from around the embroidery. Rinse the curtain in cold water until all remaining stabilizer has been removed.

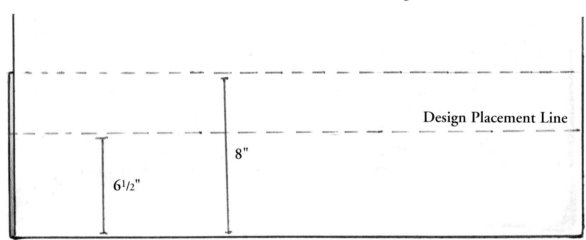

Design Placement Line

8"

6½"

Curtain Embroidery

Set the machine for embroidery:

- Feed dog down
- Embroidery needle
- Embroidery thread in needle
- Bobbin thread in bobbin *Note: Wind several bobbins before starting embroidery.*

Adhere water-soluble stabilizer to the voile using temporary fabric adhesive spray. Hoop the voile in the large oval hoop.

Trimming the Tassels

From wrong side, clip the tassels and fringing around the flowers. Carefully release threads from the front using the Embroidery Wand. For this project, do not leave any loops on the tassels or flower fringes.

Press the embroidery on the wrong side, then neaten the tassels and fringed flowers. Spray the tassels with water and straighten to remove any crinkles. Trim the tassels and fringing to remove any loops still left.

Finishing the Hem

Remove basting stitches. Using duckbill or appliqué scissors, carefully trim the raw edge of the voile from the top of the hem. Trim around the top edge of the embroidery, taking care not to cut too close to the running stitches.

Optional: Hand-stitch a flower-shaped bead above each embroidered flower, alternating the two colors as shown in the photo on page 75.

Curtain Construction

Set the machine for sewing:
- Feed dog up
- Universal needle
- Construction thread in needle and bobbin
- Reset tension if previously adjusted for embroidery

Fold under about 3/4" (2cm) along each full-length side of the panel; pin. Edgestitch along the folded edge, from the top of the panel to the lower edge. Press.

Fold under 1/2" (1.25cm) at the top edge of the panel; press. Fold under another 1 1/2" (3.75cm) hem at the top edge of the panel; pin and press.

Edgestitch the folded hem along the double-folded edge of the hem allowance.

Gather the sheer panel by threading the curtain rod through the casing.

Valance Preparation

Valance Layout & Cutting

Lay the template on the denim, close to the top edge. Trace the template three times, linking sections at sides.

Sheer Fabric Tips
- Sheer fabrics should be stitched with a shorter than normal straight stitch length–1.5mm to 2mm.
- Begin stitching 1/2" from edge, sewing a few stitches, then stitching in reverse to the edge of the seam before continuing to stitch forward. No puckers at the beginning of the stitching!
- For best results use a straight stitch plate when sewing fine and/or sheer fabrics.

Note: For a wider window, trace more sections, always centering one section and adding additional sections to each side of the middle panel.

Mark seam lines, notches and embroidery placements. *Note: Side hems are needed only on the two end panels.*

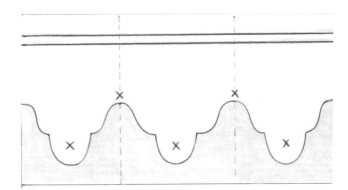

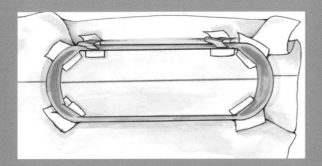

Mega Hoop Tip

The continuous border on the curtain can be stitched in a much shorter time using the Mega Hoop. Take care when hooping and clamping the fabric with the clips—to protect the voile, place a small piece of stabilizer underneath the clips as well as in the corners of the hoop. Unscrew the screws completely, hoop the voile with water-soluble stabilizer, tighten the screws halfway, carefully adjust the voile until all lines are aligned with the grid of the template, then tighten the screws completely. This will ensure that the sheer fabric will not be damaged. Make sure the hooped fabric is taut, but not distorted or pulled off-grain.

Lining Layout & Cutting

Transfer template three times as for valance, omitting the self-facing and the casing at the top edge.

Cut the lining up to the top stitching line (2); line 1 will be the new seam line.

Lining

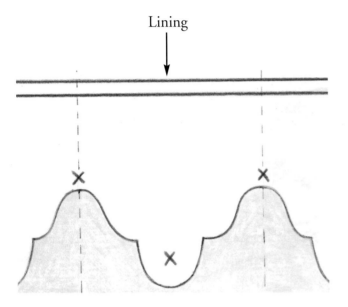

Valance Embroidery

Set the machine for embroidery:
- Feed dog down
- Embroidery needle
- Embroidery thread in needle
- Cotton bobbin thread

Hoop fabric with two layers of Lightweight Tear-Away stabilizer.

Load single flower motif #1 from Special Collection CD; enlarge 40%. Save in memory to use again later. Center the motif and embroider one flower at each of the three marked positions.

When embroidery is complete, remove fabric from hoop and remove stabilizer and unwanted threads.

Clip the flowers and tassels as described for the Sheer Panel; press and neaten tassels.

Valance Construction

Set the machine for sewing:
- Feed dog up
- Universal needle,
- Construction thread in needle and bobbin
- Piping foot (BERNINA® #12/12C) *or* zipper foot (BERNINA® #4)

Pin contrasting piping to the right side of the valance, along the seam line, starting at the left and going around the scallops to the other end. With a piping *or* zipper foot, baste the piping in place. At corners, stop with the needle down, turn, clip into the piping and continue, following the curves to the other end.

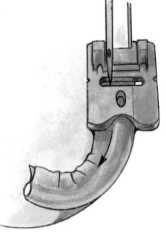

At each end, fold the piping up and away from the seam; this will eliminate excess bulk at seam ends.

On the *denim only*, fold the hem allowance A-B (two ends only) to the wrong side; press. Topstitch in place just inside the raw edge.

With right sides together, pin the valance and lining together at the top edge. Stitch across the upper edge using a 1/2" (1.2mm) seam allowance, leaving an 8" (20 cm) opening at the center for turning. Press seam toward lining.

Fold the valance self-facing toward the scallops, right sides together. Pin the lining and denim together at the two sides and around the scallops.

Stitch both side seams, beginning just below the finished casings and ending just before the piping. Backtack at beginning and end of seams.

Using a piping or zipper foot, sew around the scallops, stitching between the previous basting stitching and the piping. Grade the seams around the scallops. Clip into corners, taking care not to cut the piping. Trim unwanted threads.

Turn right side out. Neaten around the scallops. On the lining side, pin the upper edge seam opening closed. Topstitch along two marked lines, stitching through all layers. The top row of stitching will close the opening. Press the valance carefully from the back.

Valance Finishing Touch—Large Free-Hanging Tassels

Set the machine for embroidery:
- Feed dog down
- Embroidery needle
- Embroidery thread in needle
- Cotton bobbin thread

Load single tassel motif #4.

Using the tassel template, mark placement of tassels at each side of the center scallop as marked on the pattern sheet. Position tassels so the reinforcing stitches end just above the piping, as this is the thickest part of the tassel embroidery.

Adhere a layer of Stabil-Stick to the bottom of the medium hoop. Using the plastic template as a guide, place the valance on the stabilizer, centering the marked tassel location. Finger press in place.

Carefully place hoop on machine. Check position of tassel; adjust hoop position if needed.

Embroider top of tassel, using foot control to run the machine. This provides much more control, allowing embroidery to be stitched slowly, one stitch at a time!

Fold a small piece of stabilizer several times, then adhere it to the Stabil-Stick at the point where the rest of the tassel will be embroidered. This will make it easier to stitch the rest of the tassel.

Continue embroidery, completing the remaining section of the tassel. Remove from hoop; remove stabilizer and clip threads. Press from the back. Clip and trim tassels as above.

Insert brass rod into valance casing. Attach finials at each end.

chapter 10

One of the wonderful things about having a large collection of items—whether it's a collection of novelty buttons, a stash of heirloom laces, or a box full of orphan quilt blocks—is that they can be mixed and matched to create an infinite number of beautiful combinations.

Combined Collections

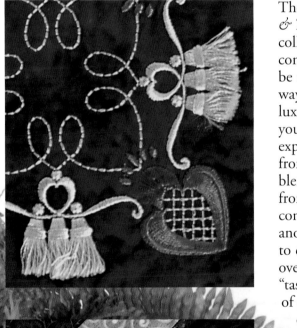

The same is true of the *Tassels & Trims* embroidery collections—all the designs complement each other and can be used together in countless ways to give any project a luxurious, rich appearance. Let yourself "out of the box"— experiment with combinations from different design groups, blending tassels and motifs from one collection with a continuous edging from another, mixing floral elements to create your own unique all-over fabric panel, or creating a "tassel sampler" by stitching one of each tassel on a single project or garment.

The Tasseled Quilt and coordinating Patchwork Pillow in this chapter are quilted and embellished with designs from all three collections. The simple Floral Scroll and Sheer Elegance designs from Collection I, beautiful

Tasseled Quilt designs from Collection II, and stately Formal Trim from the Special Collection CD all work together to make this simple quilt an exquisite work of art.

When combining disparate elements, unify them by selecting a limited color palette or by using the same types of thread throughout the project. For instance, the embroidered motifs in the Tasseled Quilt are predominately stitched in dark blue and gold Isacord embroidery thread, with additional colors selected from those in the print fabrics. Another unifying element: the background fabrics for these lovely patchwork projects are from the same collection of fabrics, beautiful prints from the Nancy's Harvest and Happy Holidays collections, designed by Nancy Halvorsen and manufactured by Benartex, Inc. (available at your local quilt shop).

Note: For a photo of the complete quilt, see page 119.

Fabric **A**   1 1/8 yards (1.03m) solid blue fabric to coordinate with florals

Nancy's Harvest collection by Benartex, *Jewel Tone Leaves*

Fabric **B**   1 3/4 yards (1.60m) blue (style 855, color 50) (includes 45" x 45" (107cm x 107cm) for backing)

Fabric **C**   1/3 yard (25.4cm) beige (style 855, color 7)

Fabric **D**   1/3 yard (25.4cm) wine (style 855, color 10)

Happy Holidays collection by Benartex, *Sugar Swirls*

Fabric **E**   1/3 yard (25.4cm) olive (style 384, color 49)

Fabric **F**   3/4 yards (66cm) gold (style 384, color 30)

45" x 45" (114cm x 114cm) square of 100% cotton batting such as Warm & Natural

Finished size of quilt—41 1/2" (102.5cm) square.

Tasseled Quilt

Worked in rich jewel tones and luxurious tassels, this small quilt is perfect for a wall hanging or as a decorative accent thrown over the back of a sofa.

Fabric Requirements
Note: Extra fabric has been allowed for hooping embroidered sections. Refer to Quilt Diagram A to see where the fabrics are used in the quilt.

Diagram A

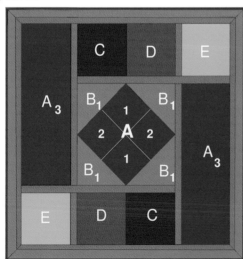

F - Sashing   **A₄** Binding   **B₂** Outer Border

Quilt Supplies
- BERNINA® Artista 200E
- BERNINA® Artista Software Designer Plus
- 1 spool blue Mettler 50 weight Silk Finish cotton thread
- 1 spool gold Mettler 50 weight Silk Finish cotton thread
- Assortment of OESD Isacord and/or Mettler Metrosheen embroidery thread
- 1 spool dark blue Mettler 40 weight cotton quilting thread
- 1 spool gold Mettler 40 weight cotton quilting thread
- 1 spool clear monofilament thread ("invisible" thread)
- Universal needles #70/10
- Quilting or Jeans needles #90/14 and #80/12 (use with monofilament)
- Embroidery needles #75/11
- Sharp or Microtex needles #80/12
- All-purpose foot (BERNINA® #1/1C)
- Machine embroidery foot (BERNINA® Foot #15)
- Machine quilting foot (BERNINA® Foot #29/29C)

Quilt Supplies (continued)

- ¹/₄" foot (BERNINA® Foot #37 or #57)
- Walking foot (BERNINA® #50)
- Edgestitch foot (BERNINA® Foot #10/10C)
- OESD Lightweight Tear-Away stabilizer
- Studio BERNINA® embroidery collections

    Tassels & Trims I–available at your local BERNINA® dealer and at www.embroideryonline.com

    Tassels & Trims II–available at your local BERNINA® dealer and at www.embroideryonline.com

    Tassels & Trims Special Collection CD included with this book

- Scissors
- Rotary cutter and cutting mat
- Quilting rulers such as Nifty Notions' Cut for the Cure 7" x 24" ruler
- Quilting pins–optional
- Masking tape
- Fabric marker–test on fabric before use
- Needle and white cotton thread for hand-basting *or*
    - 1" (2.5cm) steel safety pins if pin-basting *or*
    - Temporary spray adhesive such as 505 if spray basting
- Spray starch–optional

Cutting Tips

Note: Please follow the next steps before cutting any squares, as embroidery needs to be stitched first and extra fabric is needed for hooping.

- 10" (25.4cm) allows for extra fabric when using the large oval hoop. When using medium hoops, 9" (22.8cm) strips will be adequate for stitching smaller motifs. Lay the hoop *horizontally* on the fabric when hooping.

- Use measurements listed in the Cutting Guide. *Note: These measurements include ¹/₄" (6mm) seam allowances.* Trace these measurements on the fabric first and allow extra fabric for hooping! Cut to exact size only when all pieces have been embroidered; the lines may have to be redrawn if fabric "shrinks" during embroidery.

- Using these measurements, cut the borders, sashes and bindings crosswise in one piece. For accuracy, spray starch fabric and press before cutting the sashing and border strips.

Pieces to be Embroidered

Note: The following parts of the quilt are to be embroidered as listed below:

 A₁ On-Point Center Section–2 squares *Tassels & Trims II*, #97/83/–; reduce 20% to fit Large Oval Hoop

 A₂ On-Point Center Section–2 squares *Tassels & Trims II*, #98/84/–; reduce 20% to fit Large Oval Hoop

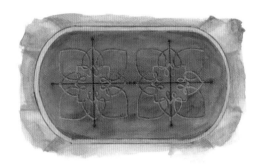

 B₁ Corner Triangles– 4 triangles *Tassels & Trims II*, #37/34/34; rotate 45° to embroider diagonally centered on triangles

 C Beige Squares–2 squares *Tassels & Trims I*, #73/66/60 as shown

 **D** Wine Squares–2 squares *Tassels & Trims I*, #73/66/60 as shown

After seaming **C** & **D** together, embroider *Tassels & Trims I* #74/67/61, two times, mirrored, centered over the seamline.

E *Tassels & Trims* Special Collection CD, #14; edit this motif by removing the tassels. Rotate the tassel top a few degrees, until it touches the left side of the heart; group. Resize, select wreath 4x, group and arrange new sewing sequence. Save; embroider in center of square. This step can only be done with the software.

A₃ *Tassels & Trims II*, #96/82/–; mirror, embroider one on each end

Tassels & Trims I, #48/41/35; rotate butterflies, embroider 4x

Tassels & Trims I, #82/–/–; embroider medallions 3x on each section

Tassels & Trims I, #65/58/52; rotate, embroider single tassel 5x on each section

Tassels & Trims I, #69/62/56; embroider two flowers on each section

Embroidery Tips

- On the lighter prints, embroider with a darker and brighter shade; on the darker prints, select lighter and brighter shades. If this method is used, the embroidery will not disappear into the print and the tassels will be effective.
- Keep the number of embroidery colors within each motif to a minimum; otherwise the quilt may appear cluttered.
- Stabilize well using tear-away stabilizer.

Cutting Guide

Cut the indicated pieces using the measurements below **after all embroidery has been stitched.** *Note: These measurements **include** ¼" (6mm) seam allowances. See diagram on previous page for fabric legend.*

Blocks

 A₁,₂ Cut 5³⁄₄" x 5³⁄₄" (14.6cm x 14.6cm) squares; cut 4

 B₁ 8¹⁄₄" x 8¹⁄₄" x 11³⁄₄" (21cm x 21cm x 30cm); cut 4
Tip: Cut two 8¹⁄₄" x 8¹⁄₄" (21cm x 21cm) squares; subcut diagonally to form two half-square triangles.

C
D 8" x 8" (20.3cm x 20.3cm); cut 6
E total (2 olive; 2 wine; 2 beige)

 A₃ 8" x 24¹⁄₂" (20.3cm x 62.2cm); cut 2

Sashing and Borders

F₁ Vertical sashing–2" x 8" (5cm x 20.3cm); cut 2

F₂ Center sashing–2" x 24¹⁄₂" (5cm x 62.2cm); cut 4

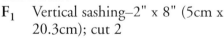

F₃ Inner border–2" (5cm) x width of fabric; cut 4

B₂ Outer border–3" (7.6cm) x width of fabric; cut 4

Binding and Backing

    A_4 Binding–3¼" (8.3cm) x width of fabric; cut 4

    A_5 Backing–45" x 45" (114cm x 114cm); cut 1

Diagram B

Assembling the Quilt

Before assembling the quilt take extra time to ensure that all the embroidered pieces are the correct shape and size. Trim if necessary.

Stitch ¼" (6mm) seams using a ¼" foot (BERNINA® Patchwork Foot #37 or Patchwork Foot with Guide #57). Press all seams to one side—no steam!

To stabilize diagonal seam lines on the triangles and mitered border seams, spray lightly with starch and press, no steam.

Refer to Quilt Diagram B for a visual of how the pieces fit together.

Diagram C

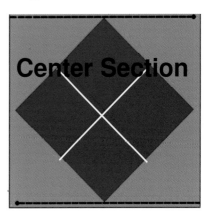

Center Section

Center On-Point Section (Diagram C)

- Join A_1 and A_2 blocks in pairs, then as one larger diamond. Press seams to one side.

- To complete the on-point center section, sew the diagonal edges of the embroidered B_1 triangles to the sides of the diamond block as shown in the diagram. Press seams—do not stretch diagonals at any time. This completes the on-point center section.

Diagram D

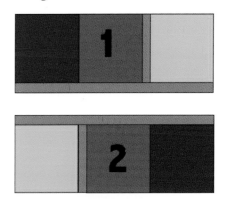

1

2

Top & Bottom Strips (Diagram D)

Note: Squares C and D were joined before the embroidery was stitched.

- Sew a short gold sashing strip to the right of the seamed **C/D** squares.

- Sew embroidered olive square **E** to the other side of gold sashing strip.

- Repeat for the remaining squares **C/D** and **E**— remember to rotate this strip. Press seams.

- Sew a long gold sashing strip to the lower side of the top **C/D/E** strip, as shown (section 1).

- Repeat for the lower **C/D/E** strip, but sew sashing strip to the top of this 3-block strip. Press seams (section 2).

Rectangle Sections (Diagram E)
Note: When joining these sections, the upper left side is higher than the lower right side in the finished quilt.

- Sew a gold sashing strip to the inside edge of both A_3 rectangles
- Press the seams to one side.

At this stage you should have five sections pieced together: two A_3 strips with gold sashing along the inner edge, two C/D/F/E with a gold sashing strip to the inside and the center "on-point section." Only the four gold border strips (F), four blue print border strips (B_2), and four binding strips (A_4) are left to sew.

Plan ahead before sewing the sections together—lay out the pieces of the quilt as they will appear in the finished piece. (Refer to Diagram F)

Diagram F

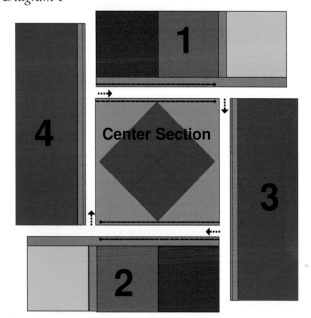

- On a large working surface lay the center section right side up.
- Lay strip 1 horizontally above the center section, right side up, aligning the raw edges on the left with the left edge of the center section.
- Lay strip 2 horizontally below the center section, aligning the raw edges on the right with the right edge of the center section.
- On the right side, place the lower blue strip 3 vertically, aligning the upper edge with the upper edge of the center section.
- Place the last blue piece, strip 4, vertically along the left side of the center section, aligning the lower edge with the lower edge of the center section. All the gold sashing strips should be along the outer edges of the center block.

Sew the four sashed strips to the four sides of the center section together in this order:
- Pin strip 1 to the top of the center section, raw edges together, aligning the left end of the strip with the left side of the center block; pin. Stitch, stopping 1/4" (6mm) from the right side of the center block (see black line in Diagram F). Backstitch to secure the end of the seam. The end of strip 1 (block E) will hang loose at the upper right side of the center block. *Note: This 1/4" (6mm) space provides room for the strip 3 seam.*
- Pin strip 2 to the lower edge of the center section, raw edges together, aligning the right end of the strip with the right side of the center block; pin. Stitch, stopping 1/4" (6mm) from the left side of the center block. Backstitch to secure the end of the seam. The end of strip 2 (olive block E) will hang loose at the lower left side of the center block.
- Fold the loose end of strip 1 to the left to reveal the seam. Pin and stitch strip 3 from the dot at the upper right corner of the center block to the outer edge of strip 2 (see red line on illustration).
- Fold the loose end of strip 2 to the right to reveal the seam. Pin and stitch strip 4 from the dot at the lower left corner of the center block to the outer edge of strip 1 (see red line on illustration).

Tip: The sides of BERNINA® Patchwork Foot #37 and Patchwork Foot with Guide #57 are marked 1/4" in front of the needle, at the needle, and 1/4" behind the needle. To eliminate the need to mark the 1/4" dots when stitching inset seams, stop stitching when the first notch reached the edge of the fabric.

The upper right and lower left **E** sections are still loose. Stitch as follows:

- Starting with strip 1, fold the loose **E** section parallel to the right, over strip 3. Stitch from the dot to the raw edge of **E**.
- Repeat for strip 2, folding **E** parallel over 4, stitching from the dot to the raw edge of **E**.
- Press the newly stitched sections in the same direction as the previously stitched seams.

Mitered Borders
A double border, of gold and blue prints, is added to the outer edge of the quilt. For this border, sew the strips together first and then attach them to the quilt as one unit.

- Join one inner border **F** with one outer border **B$_2$**. Repeat for all four border sections. Press the seams open.
- Center and pin the border strips to the quilt. Start and end the seams $1/4$" (6mm) from the raw edges. Backstitch to secure the seams. Do not trim the extended ends of the borders! These are needed for mitering the corners.
- Press the seams open. This will make stitching at 45° and creating a neat, flat mitered corner much easier.

To sew the mitered seams: *Note: Do not stretch the seams when sewing or pressing!*

- Fold the extended ends at each corner diagonally, right sides together, matching seams.
- Draw a 45° line from the quilt— through the intersection of the $1/4$" (6mm) seams at the corner— to the raw edge of the border. This marks the stitching line.

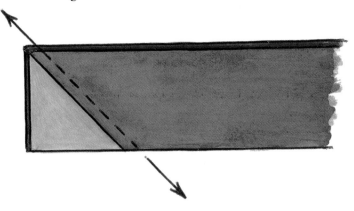

- Stitch corner. Check for squareness; press seam allowances open.
- Repeat for all four corners.

- When all four corners are finished, trim excess fabric from mitered seams.
- To ensure that the quilt and backing are still square, measure the length and width near the middle of the quilt. Use these measurements to check that the four sides of the quilt are the same.

Finishing the Quilt
- Place the backing of the quilt face down on a large, flat working surface. Smooth any wrinkles carefully by hand, then tape all sides securely to the table with masking tape.
- Place the batting on top of the backing. Smooth out any wrinkles.
- Place the quilt top right side up on top of the batting; smooth out any wrinkles. Do not stretch the quilt. Tape or pin the corners.
- Baste the three layers of the quilt together using one of the following methods:

Hand-baste, beginning in the center, spacing lines 4" (10 cm) apart until the entire quilt has been basted.

Pin-baste, beginning in the center, spacing quilting safety pins 4" (10 cm) apart until the entire quilt has been pinned.

Spray-baste, following the instructions on the can of temporary fabric adhesive.

Quilting
Stitch-in-the-Ditch
- Insert a new #80/12 Sharp or Microtex needle and attach a walking foot (BERNINA® #50) to the machine. Thread the needle with clear monofilament and fill the bobbin with gold sewing thread.
- Select straight stitch (*artista* #325) from the quilt stitch menu, or select a regular straight stitch and adjust the stitch length to 2mm.
- Sew a test sample; loosen the needle tension if necessary to produce a balanced stitch.
- Fold the quilt for easy handling under the machine.
- Starting in the center of the quilt, stitch-in-the-ditch through all layers following all the horizontal and vertical sash seam lines and triangles. *Tip: Move the needle to the far left, then guide the seam along the inside edge of the right toe of the walking foot.*

Stippling

- Attach a freemotion quilting foot (BERNINA® #29/29C) to the machine. Lower the feed dog.
- Thread the needle and bobbin with matching quilting thread.
- Before beginning, "map out" the stippling direction. Start in the center of the plain blue section and work from the top to the outside. Stipple from the top, around the first embroidery motif, up and down and around motifs without crossing over the previous stippling. Sew in a continuous line until the entire section has been covered with stippling. Start and end with a few small stitches in one place to lock the stitches.
- Repeat for the remaining blue section.

Echo Quilting

- Use the outer edge of the walking foot (BERNINA® #50) for accurate, consistent spacing of rows.
- Select a straight stitch and adjust the stitch length to 2.5mm. Use a contrasting quilting thread for the "echo" stitching.
- Following the outline of an embroidered design, stitch 3–4 rows around the designs.
- Echo quilt diamond shapes around the embroidered tassels on the center seam.
- Echo quilt half-circles around the tassels on the beige and wine print fabrics.
- Echo quilt three rows inside the four triangle sections of the center portion of the quilt.

Double Fold Binding with Squared Corners

- Trim backing and batting to match the quilt top, making sure that all the corners form 90° angles.
- Measure one side of the quilt; add 2" (5cm) to allow for finishing the binding ends. Cut the four binding strips to this length.
- Bind the two sides first and then the top and bottom edges.

  Fold the binding in half lengthwise, wrong sides together.

  Center one length of binding along one side of the quilt, extending 1" (2.5cm) at each end. Pin. Stitch binding to the quilt using a 1/4" (6mm) seam allowance. Trim ends even with the upper and lower edge of the quilt.

  Repeat for the other side of the quilt.

  Wrap each length of binding around the raw edge to the back of the quilt; pin. Blindstitch by hand

or stitch-in-the-ditch (from the front) by machine using an edgestitch foot (BERNINA® #10/10C), catching the edge of the binding in the stitching.

Center a length of binding along the upper edge of the quilt, extending 1" (2.5cm) at each end. Pin. Stitch. Trim excess length at each end to 1/2" (1.2cm); turn under the extended binding even with the quilt edges. Blindstitch by hand or stitch-in-the-ditch (from the front) by machine, catching the edge of the binding in the stitching.

Repeat for the lower edge of the quilt.

Remove all basting stitches or pins.

Sign Your Quilt

Create a custom label and attach it to the back of the quilt as desired.

Patchwork Pillow

This simple pillow echoes the patchwork and embroidery of the quilt to coordinate the décor of any room.

Finished size: 16½" x 16½" (42cm x 42cm)

Fabric Requirements

Note: Other supplies are the same as listed for the quilt on pages 82-83.

Note: Extra fabric has been allowed for hooping embroidered sections.

Fabric **A**   1/4 yard (25cm) fat quarter solid blue fabric to coordinate with florals

Nancy's Harvest collection by Benartex, *Jewel Tone Leaves*

Fabric **B**   1/4 yards (25cm) or fat quarter blue (style 85, color 50)

Fabric **C**   scrap piece wine (style 855, color 10)

Fabric **D**   scrap piece beige (style 855, color 7)

Happy Holidays collection by Benartex, *Sugar Swirls*

Fabric **E**   scrap piece olive (style 384, color 49)

Fabric **F**   1/2 yard (50cm) gold (style 384, color 30)

18" x 18" (50cm x 50cm) square of 100% cotton batting such as Warm & Natural

Embroidery

Following the general directions for the quilt, embroider and cut the pieces of the pillow using the information below.

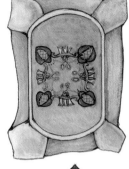

 A   On-Point Block–
1 square, *Tassels & Trims II,* #97/83; reduce 20% to fit large oval hoop

B   Corner Triangles–
2 triangles, *Tassels & Trims II,* #37/34/34; rotate 45° to embroider diagonally, centered on triangles

C   Lower Pieced Section
Tassels & Trims Special Collection, Formal Trim tassel #14 *Note: This is embroidered **after** the patchwork is complete.*

Cutting Guide

Cut the following pieces for the pillow.
Note: Position embroidery in the center of the block, avoiding seam allowances.

Blocks

 A₁   Cut 5³/₄" x 5³/₄" (14.6cm x 14.6cm) square; cut 1

 B   4¹/₂" x 4¹/₂" x 6³/₈" (11.5cm x 11.5cm x 16.3cm); cut 2. *Tip: Cut two 4¹/₂" x 4¹/₂" (11.5cm x 11.5cm) squares; subcut diagonally to form two half-square triangles*

 C
D   4³/₄" x 3¹/₄" (12.1cm x
E   8.3cm); cut 5 total (2 from olive; 1 wine; 1 beige, 1 navy)

A₂   4³/₄" x 8¹/₂" (12.1cm x 21.6cm); cut 1

Sashing and Borders

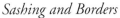 **F**   Vertical sashing–2" x 8¹/₂"
(5cm x 21.6cm); cut 1

Center sashing–2" x 14¹/₄"
(5cm x 36.3cm); cut 1

Borders–2" (5cm) x width of fabric; cut 2

Back–10" x 18"
(25.5cm x 45.5cm); cut 2

Assembly

Piece the pillow top, mitering the corners of the borders as shown in the photo. Press.

Place batting behind the pieced top and stitch-in-the-ditch along all seam lines. Stipple-quilt the upper left rectangle. Square up the pieced and quilted pillow top.

Pillow Back and Assembly

Insert zipper between the two pieces of fabric cut for the back of the pillow. Trim the back of the pillow the same size as the pieced front.

Place the pillow front and back right sides together with the zipper partially open. Stitch along all four edges using a ¹/₂" (1.2cm) seam allowance.

Trim corners, turn pillow to the right side through the zippered opening; press. Insert pillow form through the zippered opening to complete the pillow.

Key to Appendices

Tassels & Trims Collection 1	*artista* CD	*artista* card	Deco card
Diamond Braid – part 2			
	57 (3)	50	44
✳	58 (4)	51	45
	59 (5)	52	46
	60 (6)	53	47

FIRST COLUMN
- name of collection at the top of the page
- name of design group
- graphics of each design in the group

SECOND COLUMN
- *artista* 200E CD design number (example: 57 (3))
    - first number is the number of the motif
    - second number is the number of the motif within the design group
      (example: Diamond Braid folder, motif 3)

THIRD COLUMN
- *artista* embroidery card design number

FOURTH COLUMN
- Deco embroidery card design number

Note: Throughout this book, designs are indicated using all 3 numbers (example: 57/50/44). If a design is not available in a particular format, the symbol "–" appears in the column instead of a number.

Tassels & Trims Collection 1	artista CD	artista card	Deco card
Tassel Braid			
	1	1	1
	2	2	2
	3	3	3
	4	4	4
	5	5	–
Link Chain			
	6 (1)	6	–
	7 (2)	7	–
	8 (3)	8	–
	9 (4)	9	–

Tassels & Trims Collection 1	artista CD	artista card	Deco card
Scallop Braid			
	10 (1)	–	–
	11 (2)	–	–
	12 (3)	–	–
Velvet Rose			
	13 (1)	10	5
	14 (2)	11	6
	15 (3)	12	7
	16 (4)	13	8
	17 (5)	14	9

Tassels & Trims Collection 1	*artista* CD	*artista* card	*Deco* card
Crochet Braid			
	18 (1)	15	10
	19 (2)	16	11
	20 (3)	17	12
	21 (4)	18	13
	22 (5)	19	14
Daisy Heirloom			
	23 (1)	20	15
	24 (2)	21	–
	25 (3)	22	16
Royal Braid – part 1			
	26 (1)	–	–
	27 (2)	–	–
	28 (3)	–	–

Tassels & Trims Collection 1	*artista* CD	*artista* card	*Deco* card
Royal Braid – part 2			
	29 (4)	–	–
	30 (5)	23	17
	31 (6)	24	18
	32 (7)	25	19
	33 (8)	26	20
	34 (9)	27	21
	35 (10)	28	
	36 (11)	29	23
	37 (12)	30	24
	38 (13)	31	25

Tassels & Trims Collection 1	*artista* CD	*artista* card	*Deco* card
Baby Braid			
	46 (1)	39	33
	47 (2)	40	34
	48 (3)	41	35
	49 (4)	42	36
	50 (5)	43	37
	51 (6)	44	38
	52 (7)	45	39
	53 (8)	46	40
	54 (9)	47	41
Diamond Braid – part 1			
	55 (1)	48	42
	56 (2)	49	43

Tassels & Trims Collection 1	*artista* CD	*artista* card	*Deco* card
Diamond Braid – part 2			
	57 (3)	50	44
	58 (4)	51	45
	59 (5)	52	46
	60 (6)	53	47
	61 (7)	54	48
	62 (8)	55	49
	63 (9)	56	50
	64 (10)	57	51

Tassels & Trims Collection 1	artista CD	artista card	Deco card
Flower Scroll			
	65 (1)	58	52
	66 (2)	59	53
	67 (3)	60	54
	68 (4)	61	55
	69 (5)	62	56
Tassel Scallop			
	70 (1)	63	57
Sheer Elegance – part 1			
	71 (1)	64	58
	72 (2)	65	59
	73 (3)	66	60

Tassels & Trims Collection 1	artista CD	artista card	Deco card
Sheer Elegance – part 2			
	74 (4)	67	61
	75 (5)	68	–
	76 (6)	69	62
	77 (7)	70	63
Circular Braids			
	78 (1)	–	–
	79 (2)	–	
	80 (3)	–	–
	81 (4)	–	–
	82 (5)	–	–

Tassels & Trims Collection 2	artista CD	artista card	Deco card
Large Double Scallops			
	1	1	1
	2	2	2
	3	3	3
	4	4	4
Royal Lattice			
	5 (1)	5	5
	6 (2)	6	6

Tassels & Trims Collection 2	*artista* CD	*artista* card	*Deco* card
Modern Shell			
	7 (1)	7	7
	8 (2)	8	8
	9 (3)	9	9
	10 (4)	10	10
	11 (5)	11	11
Christmas Trims – part 1			
	12 (1)	12	12

Tassels & Trims Collection 2	*artista* CD	*artista* card	*Deco* card
Christmas Trims – part 2			
	13 (2)	13	13
	14 (3)	14	14
	15 (4)	15	15
	16 (5)	16	16
	17 (6)	17	17
Lilacs & Lace			
	18 (1)	18	18
	19 (2)	19	19
	20 (3)	20	20
	21 (4)	21	21

Tassels & Trims Collection 2	artista CD	artista card	Deco card
Daisy Heirloom			
	22 (1)	22	22
	23 (2)	23	23
	24 (3)	24	24
	25 (4)	25	25
	26 (5)	26	26
	27 (6)	27	27
	28 (7)	–	–
Leaf Trim			
	29 (1)	28	28
	30 (2)	29	29
	31 (3)	30	30
	32 (4)	–	–
	33 (5)	–	–

Tassels & Trims Collection 2	artista CD	artista card	Deco card
Classic Rose			
	34 (1)	31	31
	35 (2)	32	32
	36 (3)	33	33
	37 (4)	34	34
	38 (5)	35	35
	39 (6)	36	–
	40 (7)	–	–
Forget-Me-Knots – part 1			
	41 (1)	37	36
	42 (2)	38	37
	43 (3)	39	38
	44 (4)	40	39

Tassels & Trims Collection 2	*artista* CD	*artista* card	*Deco* card
Forget-Me-Knots – part 2			
	45 (5)	41	–
	46 (6)	–	–
Purple Tassels			
	47 (1)	42	40
	48 (2)	43	41
	49 (3)	44	–
	50 (4)	–	–

Tassels & Trims Collection 2	artista CD	artista card	Deco card
Hidden Hearts			
	51 (1)	45	42
	52 (2)	46	43
	53 (3)	47	44
	54 (4)	48	45
	55 (5)	49	46
	56 (6)	50	–
	57 (7)	–	–
Xtravaganza Trim			
	58 (1)	51	47
	59 (2)	52	48

Tassels & Trims Collection 2	*artista* CD	*artista* card	*Deco* card
Tassels Galore			
	60 (1)	53	49
	61 (2)	54	50
	62 (3)	–	–
Eyelet Trim			
	63 (1)	55	51
	64 (2)	56	52
	65 (3)	57	53
	66 (4)	58	54
	67 (5)	59	55
	68 (6)	–	–
	69 (7)	–	–
	70 (8)	–	–

Tassels & Trims Collection 2	artista CD	artista card	Deco card
Broken Hearts			
	71 (1)	60	56
	72 (2)	61	57
	73 (3)	62	58
	74 (4)	63	59
	75 (5)	–	–
	76 (6)	–	–
African Dreams			
	77 (1)	64	60
	78 (2)	65	61
	79 (3)	66	62
	80 (4)	67	63
	81 (5)	68	–
	82 (6)	–	–

Tassels & Trims Collection 2	artista CD	artista card	Deco card
Shades of White			
	83 (1)	69	64
	84 (2)	70	65
	85 (3)	71	66
	86 (4)	72	67
	87 (5)	73	68
	88 (6)	74	–
	89 (7)	75	–
	90 (8)	76	–
Modern Trim			
	91 (1)	77	–
	92 (2)	78	–
	93 (3)	79	–

Tassels & Trims Collection 2	artista CD	artista card	Deco card
Fantasy Trim			
	94 (1)	80	–
	95 (2)	81	–
A Tasseled Quilt			
	96 (1)	82	–
	97 (2)	83	–
	98 (3)	84	–

Tassels & Trims Collection 2	*artista* CD	*artista* card	*Deco* card
Table Linen			
	99 (1)	85	–
	100 (2)	86	–
	101 (3)	–	–
	102 (4)	–	–
Rug Tassels			
	103 (1)	–	–
	104 (2)	–	–

Tassels & Trims Special Collection CD	design #	Mega-Hoop
Flower Tassels		
	1	N
	2	N
	3	N
	4	N
ChineseTrim		
	5	N
Floral Ribbons		
	6	Y
	7	Y
	8	N

Tassels & Trims Special Collection CD	design #	Mega-Hoop
Tufted Swags		
	9	Y
	10	N
	11	N
	12	N
	13	N
Formal Trim		
	14	N
	15	N
Pretty Posies – part 1		
	16	N
	17	N

Tassels & Trims Special Collection CD	design #	Mega-Hoop
Pretty Posies – part 2		
	18	N
	19	Y
	20	N
	21	N
	22	N
Renaissance Belt		
	23	N
	24	N
Christmas Trims – part 1		
	25	N
	26	N

Tassels & Trims Special Collection CD				*design* #	Mega-Hoop
Christmas Trims – part 2					
				27	N
				28	N
				29	N
				30	N
				31	N
Chess Board – part 1					
	32	N		36	
	33	N		37	N
	34	N		38	N
	35	N		39	N

Tassels & Trims Special Collection CD				design #	Mega-Hoop
Chess Board – part 2					
	40	N		45	N
	41	N		46	N
	42	N		47	N
	43	N		48	N
	44	N			
				49	N
				50	N
				51	N
				52	Y
				53	N
				54	N
				55	N
				56	N
				57	Y

BERNINA® of America, Inc.
3702 Prairie Lake Drive
Aurora, IL 60504
www.berninausa.com

- *artista* 165E, 185E, and 200E embroidery systems
- *Deco* 650 embroidery machine
- BERNINA® presser feet and accessories
- BERNINA® *artista* and *Deco* embroidery hoops
- BERNINA® sewing machine needles
- Schmetz sewing machine needles
- Bernette® iron
- BERNINA® ironing system
- *Tassels & Trims I* embroidery collection
- *Tassels & Trims II* embroidery collection

Oklahoma Embroidery Supply & Design
12101 I-35 Service Road
Oklahoma City, OK 73131
www.embroideryonline.com

- Embroidery Collections
- *Tassels & Trims I* embroidery collection
- *Tassels & Trims II* embroidery collection
- Isacord embroidery thread
- Yenmet Metallic embroidery thread
- Mettler 60 weight cotton embroidery thread
- Mettler 50 weight Silk-Finish cotton thread
- Mettler 40 weight cotton quilting thread
- Mettler 30 weight embroidery thread
- Mettler Metrocor serger thread
- Mettler Metrolene fine thread
- YLI Monet embroidery thread
- YLI clear monofilament thread
- OESD embroidery thread
- Embroidery Wand
- OESD Tear-Away stabilizer
- OESD Cut-Away stabilizer
- OESD Aqua Mesh water-soluble stabilizer
- OESD Badgemaster heavyweight water-soluble stabilizer
- OESD Poly-Mesh cut-away stabilizer
- OESD Stabil-Stick adhesive stabilizer
- 505 temporary fabric adhesive spray
- Organ Embroidery needles

Quilters' Resource, Inc.
P. O. Box 148840
Chicago, IL 60614
www.quiltersresource.com

- Warm & Natural Quilt Batting
- Embroidery Wand
- Isacord embroidery thread
- Yenmet Metallic embroidery thread
- Mettler 60 weight cotton embroidery thread
- Mettler 50 weight Silk-Finish cotton thread
- Mettler 30 weight embroidery thread
- Mettler Metrocor serger thread
- Mettler Metrolene fine thread
- YLI Monet embroidery thread
- Embroidery Wand
- Tear-Away stabilizer
- Cut-Away stabilizer
- Aqua Mesh water-soluble stabilizer
- Poly-Mesh cut-away stabilizer
- 505 temporary fabric adhesive spray
- Nifty Notions scissors and shears
- Nifty Notions "Cut for the Cure" clear quilters rulers
- Organ Embroidery needles
- Schmetz sewing machine needles
- Helmar Fray Stoppa
- Stitch & Tear stabilizer
- HTC Pattern Ease pattern tracing fabric
- Bias tape makers, fabric markers, and other sewing notions

Benartex, Inc.
1359 Broadway, Suite 1100
New York, NY 10018
www.benartex.com

- Quilt Fabrics:
  Nancy's Harvest Collection
  Jewel Tone Leaves
  - Blue (style 855, color 50)
  - Wine (style 855, color 10)
  - Beige (style 855, color 7)
  Happy Holidays Collection
  Sugar Swirls
  - Olive (style 384, color 49)
  - Gold (style 384, color 30)

Miscellaneous

Plaid® Mod Podge™—Available at your local craft store

Candle Podge by Silk Art · P. O. Box 1609 · Durbanville 7551 · South Africa

Clear Silicone Sealant, such as Marine Goop or Dap—Available at your local hardware store

Bold indicates photo.

Appendix noted in parenthesis as
such: (B) = Appendix B.

Tabletop Ballerina

Chapter 7

Overlay Appliqué Table Topper

Chapter 8

Tasseled Quilt & Patchwork Pillow
Chapter 10

Sheer Christening Dress

Chapter 8